The Success Solution

Break Through Limiting Beliefs for Business Success

by Loren Fogelman

ISBN: 978-0-9852900-2-3

Printed in the United States of America.

Edited by Jessica Vineyard, Red Letter Editing, LLC

www.redletterediting.com

Important Note

The Emotional Freedom Technique (EFT) and Meridian Tapping Therapies (MTT) are part of Energy Therapy. EFT and MTT are relatively new and still considered to be experimental in nature. Many people have experienced long-lasting relief from these techniques. The information provided here is to inspire, motivate, and stimulate your creativity.

This EFT/MTT-oriented product is provided as a good faith effort to expand the use of EFT in the world. It represents the ideas of EFT practitioner Loren Fogelman and do not necessarily represent those of EFT founder Gary Craig or EFT. While EFT has been used by thousands of therapists, nurses, social workers, psychologists, doctors, and individuals worldwide with exceptional results and minimal negative side effects, this does not mean that you will not experience any side effects. If you use EFT/MTT on yourself or others, you are advised to take full responsibility for yourself and the treatment

EFT/MTT does not replace traditional therapy, counseling, or medical treatment. Consult with your health care professional prior to making changes in your lifestyle, diet, exercise routine, or medication.

Loren Fogelman provides these materials as an EFT Advanced Certified Practitioner. Loren is **not** a licensed mental health therapist or medical health care provider. Her unique approach includes the core EFT principles.

Contents

Introduction

The last time you failed, what happened? Did you get discouraged? Did you beat yourself up? Did you consider throwing in the towel? If so, you might have missed an opportunity for a breakthrough.

The truth is, failure is necessary for success. If you are not failing, you are not taking risks. And if you are not taking risks, you are not going to reach your full potential. The intention is not to avoid failure, but to approach it as an opportunity in disguise. Exactly how to do that is one of the many tools I will teach you in this book.

As you will see, I walk my talk. When it feels right, I will go against the grain and be bold. It is probably one of the reasons I felt like a black sheep as I was growing up. In fact, if you had told me at age twelve that one day I would be teaching entrepreneurs how to reach their full potential, I would have said you were crazy. I wasn't a natural-born leader. Throughout my school years, I was always one of the picked-on kids in the class. I wasn't popular, athletic, or talented. In fact, school was socially torturous. I was much more at home in the library.

Like many kids who are not part of the in crowd, I didn't realize there was more to being on the social fringes than what I perceived. I also didn't realize that a burning desire to follow my purpose could be kindled and emerge suddenly, as it did, taking me by surprise in my forties.

That is how old I was when I traded my comfortable city lifestyle and we moved across the country from Miami, Florida, to Ashland, Oregon. Over the years, I *had* learned to disregard popular opinion and to pursue my passion: I was a stay-at-home mom for nine years, I started a photography business specializing in birthing, and I became a competitive rower, although I never played competitive sports in school.

Given the passion that photography has kindled in my work and life, my clients are often surprised to learn how necessity disrupted that course. My husband, Steve, got me into photography. It was an activity we shared. When we moved from the city to the country, I expected to pursue my photography career. Ashland offered a rich assortment of culture and the arts.

I developed ties to the arts community, and several galleries exhibited my work during our first year in our new community. It was a lot of fun, and I kept expanding my network.

When we moved to Oregon, we bought an existing counseling agency. Within the first six months, it was obvious that Steve needed my help. I hadn't worked as a therapist for nine years and never imagined returning to the field.

Steve and I were running our own counseling agency with eleven employees. It wasn't long, though, before I realized I couldn't juggle work, family, and photography. I was pulled in too many directions. The decision was very difficult, but I decided to put my camera on a shelf.

I developed a personal philosophy that I have used on myself and with my clients. I believe that I have not been given any challenges in my life I can't rise up to and overcome—even when I chose those challenges myself. We all can overcome incredible obstacles as long as we don't give up.

I mourned putting my photography business on hold, as it nourished the creative part of my being. Six years after that decision, I realized how my creativity continued to flourish.

One single insight shifted my entire perspective: my creativity was part of my therapy practice. My clients benefit because I am innovative and seek to transform a negative into a positive.

Several years later, a new challenge arose. I loved helping my clients get unstuck, but the spark to continue as a therapist had dwindled. I wasn't challenged any longer and yearned to rekindle my passion. I started to search for something different, something that emphasized people's potential instead of a disease model. This new path led me to discover energy psychology.

Energy psychology changed my life, and as I started to learn it, I was pleasantly surprised to discover my passion once again. Chakras, meridians, and auras were the missing links to my therapy practice. Energy work, however, was still foreign to me. My years of education didn't introduce me to this way of thinking, but I kept at it and stretched myself in ways I didn't know I could.

As with any professional seeking to make a difference with their clients, I discovered that energy psychology demanded I face my limiting thoughts and beliefs that created doubt about how it all works.

Luckily, I had some strategies for approaching my apprehension. Since 1985, I had helped my clients overcome their fears and change the belief systems that held them back at work or in their relationships. I had developed a reputation for quick results—sometimes after only one session—so I was determined to give myself the benefit of my own skill. I adopted a "no-excuses" approach and began working on my mindset.

One of the biggest obstacles holding me back was my New York attitude, my skepticism. It is true that energy psychology is a paradigm shift away from the disease model. Attending a local seminar on the topic and actually seeing it practiced for the first time made me even more skeptical. How could a bunch of tapping on various parts of the face and body eliminate lifelong beliefs?

This information was pushing me out of my comfort zone, and I was hindered by the limiting beliefs I didn't even know I had. One of the things that helped me move forward was deciding to "become comfortable being uncomfortable," a business marketing concept, and one that I have lived by since I was a little girl. I decided to apply it to my therapy practice, embracing the motto: "If it's uncomfortable, then I ought to be doing it."

My motto gave me permission not only to face my fears but to actively seek them out so I could clear them. I committed to doing whatever was necessary to work toward my business-related desires.

I was determined to break those limiting, self-imposed barriers, some of which were focusing on conventional therapy practices.

Your Mindset and Focus

In order to overcome my skepticism, I had to change my mindset and focus. By "mindset," I mean my beliefs and perceptions. I needed to become aware of my limiting beliefs. I also began reframing obstacles into opportunities. To "reframe" means to change the way you perceive something. You see it through a different set of lenses, from a different perspective.

One opportunity to do that came about as I faced having to take the indoor rowing test, which was required every year in order to be able to row on the racing team. It was something I dreaded.

The angst I had about taking the test was only adding to my struggle. I had thoughts such as, "I can't do this." Also, the first time I took the test, I got halfway into it and was thinking, "Oh, my God, how can I do this for another two and a half minutes!"

Those thoughts didn't help, so the next year I decided to train with a world-class rower, Andy Baxter, to improve my technique and tap into his winning mindset. While training with him physically, I also worked on my mental game, dredging up anything and everything that was getting in my way.

Using the tools I used on my business clients, I changed my mindset—the way I was thinking. Instead of saying, "I can't do it," I started saying, "I can do anything for two and a half minutes."

That simple shift to "I can do anything for X amount of minutes" had a profound effect on me and helped with races, as well. My focus went from *I can't* to *Yeah, I can! Bring it on!*

I actively used visualizations and tapping (EFT, or Emotional Freedom Technique, a very simple technique I will explain in chapter 6). Also, since memories are reinforced through emotion and we tend to remember jingles, I created some jingles around rowing to help with my mindset shift.

Those techniques created a paradigm shift, which is the purpose of the work I do with my clients. My work is not about adding to what they do but about clearing the gunk, getting rid of the negative clutter, those self-defeating thoughts, and changing the impact their story has on them so that they have the clarity of *Yes! I can do that.*

When you apply my method to your business, you will discover the quick and significant results that implementation and mindset can bring. Like the equation $1+1=3$, together the two modalities create dynamic results far greater than either could alone.

What Is Possible for You

Sometimes we create a goal for ourselves that is so big or meaningful that we talk ourselves out of it, because what if it doesn't happen? What would that say about us? What would it mean?

If you have the goal, you can accomplish it. Remember, you are not given any challenges you can't overcome; therefore, it becomes a matter of perspective. Consider the start-up entrepreneurs who were told, "You've gotta be kidding. You want to do that?" and then went on to defy the odds. They did so because they were so committed to their vision that they actively looked for opportunities and saw obstacles as just another challenge to get through, whereas another person might walk away from his or her dream.

A perfect example is the idea that we can power our technology devices without cords. The tech industry claimed that recharging our devices requires us to plug into a power outlet. They said wireless recharging wasn't possible, that it defied the laws of physics and would never work. Meredith Perry, the founder of uBeam, didn't believe them and started searching for a way to bring wireless power to the world.

The uBeam product, which has not yet come to market, harnesses the power of ultrasound, and as of this writing, Apple is expected to build wireless charging technology into its iPhone 8. As this shows, limiting beliefs are not held only by individuals. We can all have them and can perceive them as truth when they are actually just based upon perception and rationale. There is usually some logic to back up the particular belief, but as I discuss later, logic goes only so far.

When Meredith Perry researched long-range wireless charging, she broke a technology barrier that has the potential for far-reaching impact. In this book, I will teach you how to break the barriers in your mind. I will share with you simple yet powerful ways to shift the way you think so you can be freed from the doubts, worries, and fears that are holding you back.

Some of what you read may sound strange at first. It may sound too simple, too easy. I, too, was skeptical at first that something as simple as "tapping" could have an effect, but I tested it, and the results spoke for itself.

I will close with that story because it illustrates how small changes in thinking can have far-reaching results.

How EFT Changed My Life and Work

Before I went out on my own, I felt that some nugget was missing from my counseling practice, so I started exploring other approaches. When I became aware of energy psychology, I felt like I had found the missing link.

Despite my initial enthusiasm, at the first EFT workshop I attended, I was a complete skeptic. It was so far removed from anything I had ever seen before, and I just couldn't see how tapping on your body while saying some words could work. But I didn't fully discount it and took the manual home.

Several months later, when we were going to visit my family in Florida for the holidays, I decided to try EFT on myself to curb my desire for sugar and chocolate, which I had struggled with all my life. Every morning and afternoon for ten days, I went into the bathroom where no one could see me, and I "tapped."

Two things came out of it. I ate much less chocolate and sugar than usual, and to my astonishment, my allergies disappeared. Growing up in Florida, I had lived on allergy medications, and when I used to visit family there, within one or two days, I would be miserable. But this time, I had no allergy symptoms at all.

On the plane on the way back home, I decided that I wasn't going to eat chocolate or sugar anymore—my desire was just not there—and I haven't had sweets since 2006. That was amazing to me at the time because controlling my sugar intake had been a lifelong struggle, and being able to walk away from it so easily was surprising.

Later I learned that the foods you crave are an energetic allergy. Because I was tapping for the energetic allergy to chocolate, I was actually correcting my energy system around allergies in general without realizing it. Also, since 2006, I haven't had any allergy symptoms at all.

After those results, I started doing EFT with a client, an actor who wanted to move up to better parts in his company. I found that a core incident that was holding him back occurred in his senior year during a football game when the ball was thrown to him and slipped through his fingers. It was the final seconds of the final game of the season, and he was blamed when the team lost the district title. As a result of our work together on this one incident, his fear of "missing a line" went away. He started to have more acting work than he could handle, *and* his golf game improved.

Inspired by those results, I tried EFT with a personal fitness trainer who was experiencing a lot of anxiety before a CrossFit competition. I helped her see how her need to win was interfering with her performance. We worked with it, and after only one session, we were able to get to the heart of her anxiety and completely eliminate it. At the competition the following weekend, she faced her toughest competitor and later reported that she had had a blast throughout the competition and came in first place for the series.

Once I had personally experienced these results, I knew I had to share what I had learned. I started to work with entrepreneurs, talented and dedicated individuals who were holding themselves back, thinking they just had to tough it out, and didn't realize that change can occur easily.

Since those early results, I have worked with thousands of private clients, spoken in front of groups, gotten great results on radio shows, and developed my Business Success Solution, which I am teaching you in this book. Here is the bottom line: You don't have to struggle, and you already know how to be great.

My work is about helping you get past your barriers, achieve freedom, and easily access your inner potential. I won't be happy until you reach your top goal, whether it is building an online or a brick and mortar business or getting recognized as a thought leader and change agent in your industry. If you have that vision, you can get there.

When you opt into the bonus section online, you will have access to various references about EFT. The bonus handouts and videos are available at http://BusinessSuccessSolution.com/book-bonus.   Now let's get started.

Part One:
Unleash Your Brilliance

1. Where Do You Want to Be?

How big is your vision? What goal have you set for yourself? Do you want to be locally successful or develop an international business or rise to the top of your industry as the go-to expert? Do you daydream about it? Do you see yourself succeeding?

I have good news for you. If you can dream about being a successful entrepreneur, then it is possible to actually be there. I am not talking about hocus pocus or magic. I am talking about the power of your mind and the strength of your convictions.

The first step to realizing your vision is to learn how to think like a successful business owner. Your success mindset will not only boost your confidence, it will help to advance your business.

How a Success Mindset Pays Off

Highly successful entrepreneurs think differently from everyone else about the way they do business. When you are growing your business, educate yourself about the common characteristics and habits of successful entrepreneurs. Since success is 90 percent mindset—meaning how you think—it is clear that a success mindset can make the difference.

Too many entrepreneurs neglect their mindset, which leads to inefficiency and distraction. When you are rising to the top, you need all the energy and concentration you can muster for optimal results. You want to be laser focused on your vision, the service you offer. Expending energy on distractions such as self-critical thoughts is wasting your valuable resource.

Success mindset development begins with getting rid of the gunk, understanding where those negative thoughts come from, and working to free yourself from their grip. Yes, it is possible, but commitment is needed. A success mindset is learned.

As you evolve, you gain mental and emotional endurance and become stronger, more flexible, responsive, and resilient. Those are the key ingredients for successfully growing your business. Entrepreneurs lacking in these qualities go only so far before negative thoughts creep in and stop them. But when your focus is strong and unwavering and you can do what is necessary without making it personal, you will see significant results with your business.

We have been told about the importance of muscle memory. Repetition strengthens the neuropathways in the brain that electrical signals follow, which in turn causes muscle groups to respond. The same thing happens with your mindset. Your new techniques build neuropathways in the brain that become second nature to follow when it is time to stretch beyond your current comfort levels.

Why Mindset Is Necessary

Many people say they want to be successful with their business, but it doesn't happen. Why? Underneath their words, in their subconscious minds, are values or beliefs that are contradictory to success. These beliefs are often unknown to the person because they were adopted from the adults surrounding them before they were able to reason, before about age seven.

We also form subconscious beliefs from the experiences we have. For instance, if a child watches his parents struggle financially and hears them discuss money as something that is bad, the child develops beliefs about himself and his relationship to money. He may believe that money means "a dollar's work for a dollar's pay" and that there is never enough. Even if he later becomes a business owner, those old beliefs are still underneath, interfering with his every attempt to achieve financial freedom. He may say all the right things to himself, but he also holds his business back, gets distracted easily, or gets overwhelmed, and he doesn't understand why.

When your words and your conscious thoughts are not in alignment with the values and beliefs in your subconscious mind, incongruency occurs and a struggle develops. The subconscious mind always wins the struggle.

On the other hand, when your values and beliefs match the things you say, there is congruency, and you can then excel at whatever you choose to do. Have you ever been determined to do something your way even though everyone else had doubts, and you succeeded? That is congruency. One of the tricks for consistent congruency, which I discuss in subsequent chapters, is to ferret out the beliefs you are not aware of so that you can work to be free of them.

Your Big Why

In the rest of this chapter, we are going to focus on strengthening your conscious mind, the thoughts you *are* aware of. Part of that is encouraging you to dream big. Another part is to discover your motivation to excel. What is your *Big Why*?

In other words, what drives you to succeed? Why are you committed to achieving your full potential and growing your business? I want you to understand the driving force motivating you to keep going even when someone else tells you to quit. That motivation is different for each person.

External and Internal Motivators

Often, people start their own business because something motivated them and an opportunity was created. Originally, an *external motivator* arose—the motivation was outside of them rather than within. Then, as the idea grew, they recognized a personal reason to start a business. They developed their own *internal motivation*, which means that they were connected to *why* they were starting a business.

External factors can get you started as an entrepreneur, but they don't have enough power to keep you committed if, for instance, those factors are not truly aligned with your values. An example is the accountant working in the family business because his father expects that from him, but deep in his heart he would rather be playing music. Eventually, he is going to regret not pursuing his passion.

External motivations also are not strong enough to keep you going when circumstances become difficult. You may be great at the service you provide, but if you never connect to your internal motivation, once your external motivation is gone and you hit a rough patch, you will likely walk away.

Internal motivation, on the other hand, promotes long-lasting success. Your Big Why is an internal motivator. When you connect to your Big Why, you are driven to excel, ready to go the distance despite obstacles that appear along the way. It is as though you have a flame burning inside of you, igniting you to reach your goal.

Many entrepreneurs love what they do. A client of mine admits she would continue to help others even if she wasn't getting paid. Making a difference by sharing her gifts is what drives her to continue building her business, day in and day out.

My internal motivation is to be the best I can be. I tend to be highly driven, and I always want to be a student first, increasing what I know and stretching myself. That was my motivation for stepping away from our counseling agency, where I was working side by side with my husband, and eventually becoming a business coach.

What drives you in your business? What keeps you going when you face obstacles?

Connecting with Your Big Why Is Crucial

If you don't connect with your Big Why, eventually you will give up, burn out, or claim that your dream was not "meant to be."

For instance, if you have friends or family who are critical of you and you are not connected to your Big Why, eventually you can get beaten down by the criticism, believe in their negativity, and throw in the towel. On the other hand, if you are connected to what drives you in your business, you can find the fight in yourself to prove those people wrong.

Your Big Why can keep you going no matter what. Excuses disappear. Your full potential becomes unleashed.

Knowing the reason you are committed to being an entrepreneur is a powerful resource that no one can take away from you. It is an unstoppable force that gives you meaning, strength, and motivation. A deep inner drive propels you forward even when everyone else has given up.

When you connect to your Big Why, you become more dedicated to succeeding, willing to make significant changes such as leaving people behind, and modifying your work-life balance.

Part of what kept me from transitioning from my work as a therapist to business coaching for more than a year was that I just couldn't see myself doing it on my own without Steve. Eventually, however, my desire to move in this direction became stronger than my resistance to the sacrifices I would have to make, and I became willing to make the commitment.

Some entrepreneurs naturally connect to their Big Why, but *deciding* to do so is also possible. If you haven't already, will you make that decision now?

An Exercise to Help You Connect with Your Big Why

Think back to when you first started your profession. What did you love about it? How did it feel when you realized what you were capable of doing? Why did you decide to give everything you had to follow this path?

Or think of a time when you faced an obstacle in your business. Perhaps someone was opposing you or criticizing you. Perhaps you were faced with an uncomfortable decision to make. What did you tell yourself to keep going despite the obstacle? What was your motivation to continue despite the odds?

On the lines below, write down three to five of those things. They are the makings of your Big Why.

Be honest, even if your motivation wasn't positive. Sometimes an entrepreneur is driven not by a desire to succeed but a desire to not fail. For example, a life coach I did EFT with highly valued owning a business because his parents were successful business owners. He felt their pride when he achieved milestones and disappointment when he failed. For him, entrepreneurship wasn't about succeeding but about not failing and not disappointing his parents. He had the goal to succeed and his business grew, but because his motivation was not failing, a struggle ensued, and he eventually burned out.

If you identify with that story, you are being honest, which is good. This is just the kind of subconscious material that this book can help you clear out. Once you do that, you can connect to something deeper, an internal motivator that can truly carry you to the fulfillment of your dreams. This exercise is available at http://BusinessSuccessSolution.com/book-bonus.

My Big Why
1. My 3 to 5 motivators are:

_____

_____

_____

_____

_____

2. Are the motivators positive or negative?

If one or more of your motivations are negative, you can change them and turn them around.

Here is a process, based on Byron Katie's *The Work*, for turning a negative motivation into a positive one:

1. If your Big Why contains a negative statement, is it true? If an entrepreneur is driven "not to fail," an example of their negative statement might be, "I don't want employees."
2. Is this the only way to look at the situation?

3. When you think about that negative statement, what do you notice? Is there a certain sensation in your body or a change in energy?

4. How would your focus be different if you didn't have that negative thought? Spend some time with this question. Let yourself imagine all the ways.

5. Now rephrase your statement to make it positive. For example, instead of your goal being something you don't want to do, for example, "Don't hire employees," you would make it a positive statement such as "Find reliable help."

6. Make your positive goal as specific as possible. Modify "Find reliable help" to "Hire a trustworthy employee who shares my vision, so I can spend more time with my clients doing the activities I enjoy most."

Now, instead of a negative motivator, which encourages avoidance, you have a specific, positive motivator that will set you up for success. If you are used to motivating yourself in negative ways, positive motivators may be uncomfortable at first, but they will support you better over the length of your career.

The Gap

You know where you want to go, and now you know *why* you want to get there. The question is: Why aren't you there yet? This is where your mindset truly begins it work.

The space between where you are now and where you would like to be is called "the gap." All entrepreneurs driven toward excellence possess a gap.

For instance, a dedicated bookkeeper I worked with was driving all across the city to see her clients, but that was exhausting. Her desire to work closely with her clients was creating too much driving time for her.

We had to uncover the core reason about why driving to see her clients mattered so much to her, and she discovered that it was because close relationships with her clients were so important to her. How else could she maintain those close relationships besides driving so much? We developed a list of alternative options, and renting an office where she could regularly meet with her clients topped the list. But she wondered how her clients would react to this change. Would they get upset with her or question her decision? Those concerns had to be addressed first.

Perhaps you want to reach a larger audience or raise your industry standards or innovate a new program, but you keep missing the mark or are just not there yet. The gap is between where you are and where you want to be.

Once you commit to your goal and recognize your gap, little steps to help you close it will begin to appear. Some of these stepping stones might have been there all along, but you just never noticed them because your focus was elsewhere.

For example, an author was preparing for her first speaking and book signing tour. As you can imagine, that is a significant undertaking. She got nervous as soon as she agreed to the cross-country tour, realizing what she had committed to and needing reassurance of her capabilities.

The capability was in her; she just didn't see it at first. I helped her tap into the qualities and commitment level that had helped her to successfully rise up to a big goal she had achieved earlier in her life. Those qualities were her stepping stones, revealing to her that she had the necessary capabilities to engage with her audience and followers. Knowing it was within her because she had already done it once gave her the confidence to take it on.

How Do You Bridge the Gap?

The difference between successful entrepreneurs and everyone else boils down to one thing: how you choose to bridge the gap.

Your approach to the gap is determined by your beliefs, perceptions, prior experiences, and support system. The most successful entrepreneurs take imperfect but decisive action to close the gap. They continue to make progress toward the next level of achievement while correcting their course along the way. The gap is not a problem, it is an opportunity.

Many entrepreneurs make the mistake of focusing on where they are now, what is right in front of them. Although the day-to-day business operations have to continue, you must remain focused on your goal, your vision. This is where your reason to excel comes in.

Connecting to your Big Why will help you return your focus to your goal.

Before you can bridge the gap, you must first discover what it looks like for you. The following exercise will help you do that.

An Exercise to Help You Discover and Cross the Gap

Take a step back from where you are now. Think about your Big Why, about what motivates you to excel. Really drink it in.

Now, connect with the excitement and anticipation you feel as you imagine yourself as a success, as you see the people you have helped along the way, knowing you have made a difference for them. Tap into that feeling of success and achievement.

How will you, professionally, personally, or spiritually, be different once you reach your peak?

Write down five things about your development and the achievements you will accomplish.

Where I want to be:

1._____

2._____

3._____

4._____

5._____

Now consider your current business. Where are you now? Where aren't you getting the results that you want? Under what circumstances do you get frustrated? What challenges have affected your vision? How do you deal with unforeseen circumstances? What are some of the thoughts that go through your head?

Write down five of those things now.

Where I am:

1._____
2._____
3._____
4._____
5._____

You now have a solid picture of your gap. You know where you are and where you want to be. The next step is to cross it.

Having a tool for crossing the gap is important because entrepreneurs can get stuck as they encounter their gap. They may give up, and it doesn't have to be that way. With the proper tools and a little support, you have what you need to get where you want to go.

As I lead you through the various ways to cross the gap, I want you to approach the process like a child. Here is what I mean.

When adults want to change a behavior, they believe they need to break an old habit first, whereas children just start something new.

Trying to break an old habit takes a lot of energy and keeps you focused on what you are not doing well. What you focus on expands, so not only are you wasting energy by trying to break a habit, you are focusing on the wrong thing.

When you approach change as a child, you are ready to try new things to find a better way. You move forward without any drag from the past.

As you read the options below, think of them as helpful tools and new habits to adopt. No tool is better than another. The one you are willing to use is the one that is right for you.

Tools for Crossing the Gap

Use reverse engineering. My personal favorite approach for crossing the gap is to develop a plan from my future goal back to the present. This is called "reverse engineering." Along the way, you create milestones. Those are the destinations of where you want to be by specific dates. Consider the steps you need to take to reach each milestone. This becomes your action plan.

Studies show that writing down your goal improves your chances for success, so let's do that right now. What would you like to accomplish by next year? Choose one goal. Then we will work the timeline backward.

1. One year from now I would like to accomplish

_____

_____

2. This is where I will be in nine months:

_____

_____

3. My six-month milestone is

_____

_____

4. My ninety-day progress toward my goal is

_____

_____

5. In thirty days, I will be doing these things as I work toward my one-year goal:

_____

_____

You now have an action plan for crossing the gap. This activity is available at

http://BusinessSuccessSolution.com/book-bonus.

Be creative. This process can be applied by both the cognitive planner and the creative thinker. Many tools are available in this category. Whatever your style, there is something for you.

One tool is a **vision board**, which typically is a collage of pictures and words cut out from magazines that represent where you want to be, creating a visual representation of your goal. It creates a picture in your mind, boosting the power of your written goals. Your vision board includes words and pictures that have meaning for you. When you look at it, you become inspired by what is possible.

Be sure to put on your vision board the date by which you wish to accomplish your goal. Place your collage where you are likely to see it often so that you are inspired to keep crossing the gap. I keep mine in my bedroom by my dresser. I look at it first thing in the morning and right before I go to bed.

Other tools include **calendars, mind mapping**, and **flow charts**.

By far the best **calendar** I have found for goal setting is the Google Calendar. It is user friendly and can by accessed by any device via the Internet. Take the milestones you created in the above exercise and put them on your Google Calendar.

What makes Google Calendar so easy is that different types of activities can be color-coded for easy tracking. You can set two different colors for tactical and mindset milestones, for example. The activities to reach these milestones can also be added to your calendar with individualized colors. Say you are working on a goal to get beyond your fear of speaking. Within ninety days, you want three speaking engagements on your calendar. That ninety-day milestone could be color-coded blue. You also have committed to using visualization to reduce your fear of public speaking twice a week. You will visualize yourself speaking to a group of your ideal clients and see yourself maintaining a positive perspective. (This is addressed in chapter 6.) The days you use visualization are color-coded green. Your tactical goals might be orange, and their corresponding activities in yellow.

To learn about **mind mapping**, check out the excellent video tutorial by its creator, Tony Buzan. As of this writing, it is available here: http://www.youtube.com/watch?v=MlabrWv25qQ.

Flow charts are a wonderful tool for linear thinkers who love to follow a step-by-step plan, see how the different steps are connected, and know the important decisions along the way. As of this writing, this Web page gives a comprehensive explanation of flow charts for reaching a goal:

http://www.mindtools.com/pages/article/newTMC_97.ht m.

Whichever tool you choose, follow through. Keeping a plan in place to follow action steps and track progress increases your success rate. Consider trying two different tools to challenge both your right and left brain. You might be surprised by the results.

Choose a buddy. If you realize you are getting off track with your schedule or you are distracting yourself or making excuses, get an accountability buddy. Having another like-minded entrepreneur whom you see or check in with on a regular basis is powerful. It helps you to maintain focus and keeps you on course.

Your buddy might be another entrepreneur who is in the same field or someone you talk with regularly. There are benefits to both types. When you talk with your buddy, your check-ins should not be long conversations that go over your business strategy. They should be brief five-minute talks, stating your intentions and goals for the day. They are designed to keep you accountable to your vision.

Hint: Whichever type of buddy you select, be strategic about your choice. Look for someone who is operating their business at a higher level than you are. This challenges you to improve. You will also observe how business owners at a higher level of proficiency think, strategize, and perform. This will expand your awareness and set you up for the next level of success.

In this chapter, we have been working with your conscious mind, the thoughts you are aware of, to help you think like a success. That is only part of the process. In the next chapter, we address your subconscious mind, the part of you that is responsible for most of your actions and results.

2: The Inner Struggle

A success mindset is all about your attitude. It is about how you perceive something, and how you perceive something is determined by your experiences, the meanings you gave to your experiences, and the beliefs you created from those experiences.

Even though most people never consider questioning their beliefs, the good news is that things can change. Beliefs, perceptions, and even your subconscious mind can be altered. You can become conscious of what drives you and of your inner struggle, and you can change it all.

How Do You Perceive Setbacks?

When faced with a setback, are you the type to go with the flow or to resist? Is your first response defeat, feeling as though you will never reach your goal? Do you see your setback as a failure?

Setbacks can actually set the stage for breakthroughs if you perceive them in a positive light, but too often we view them negatively, as failures. When you view setbacks in a negative way rather than as obstacles everyone faces or, preferably, as challenges, you become focused on what is not working well. Fear, doubt, worry, and overwhelm set in. You start to experience what I call a "breakdown."

For instance, if you have a goal and you are not where you expected to be, you may find yourself using a lot of negative self-talk. If you are concerned about what others think, you may wonder if you are worthy of accepting challenging projects. What if you are in a leadership position and decision-making is difficult? You might be concerned that you are letting your clients down and become very hard on yourself. Slipping into a negative mindset, where you beat yourself up, is too easy.

Whatever you focus on expands, so if you are focusing on where you are not yet and on the problems, seeing solutions is difficult. You could be missing opportunities. Focusing on the problem also creates a struggle and a self-fulfilling prophecy. You begin to doubt yourself. Your confidence wanes.

Doubt is like a cancer. Once the seed of doubt gets planted in your mind, your ego, which actually wants to keep you where you are, recognizes the fear, feeds on it, and the fear expands—you break down.

How to Break Through

When you understand that a breakdown *always* occurs prior to a breakthrough, you can begin to turn the situation around. Not only does your perspective change, but your response changes, as well. Instead of losing confidence, you begin to view the setback as just one more hurdle on your way to growing a successful business. Take a moment and consider that. When you begin to train your mindset to switch from focusing on the problem to discovering solutions, your response changes. Instead of viewing situations as barriers, you view them as challenges to overcome. There is nothing like a good challenge to spark a growth-minded entrepreneur's desire to excel.

Too often, however, a breakdown will stop entrepreneurs because they are too identified with their egos. When I refer to the ego, I mean the part of us whose primary job is to keep us safe. Unfortunately, the ego tries to keep us safe by preventing us from actually taking risks and pushing ourselves. It can't discriminate between positive risk and negative risk, and views all risk as unsafe.

The doubts, fears, and worries you experience are created by the ego as it attempts to keep you where you are. Its perspective appears very, very real. It is the source of your resistance.

Among other things, your ego is concerned with your image and how other people perceive you, external factors you are unable to control. Your ego is highly judgmental.

The more you move past your doubts and fear and continue to push yourself despite them, the less you are in need of your ego—and the last thing the ego wants is extinction, so it raises the alarm even more. How? By causing you to experience more doubt and by bringing in guilt and shame.

Rather than trying to extinguish the ego and thus setting the stage for an internal battle to the death, aim instead for transformation. Become aware of your thoughts and emotions, and then change your response. Instead of believing you have to "do" something because you are feeling a certain way, just observe your emotions.

See if you can acknowledge or name what you are feeling. You are much more complex than happy, sad, bored, or angry. You don't need to do anything else. You don't have to try to change the feeling. Eventually, it will change on its own.

I know this seems counterintuitive because we are so conditioned to respond, but give it a try for one week and see how it is to note your emotions, whether fear, doubt, or worry, and to not act on them. The choice is yours: act or react.

How to Transform the Ego Response

When I work with clients, we first identify their fears, doubts, and worries, find out where they came from, and what their purpose is, and then I look at how the client can take the underlying qualities of the ego response and use them in a positive way, in partnership.

For example, if you are experiencing a lot of fear and feel stuck, you may discover that, because of things that happened to you in childhood, your ego created a strong internal protector that is always on the lookout for danger. The problem is that your protector can keep you from taking reasonable risks.

Risks come in all varieties. I am not suggesting you do something that would put you in a dangerous situation. I am encouraging you to step out of your comfort zone and challenge what you believe you are capable of doing. Stretching your perception about your capabilities leads to actually expanding your abilities.

Rather than fighting the ego, begin to think of it as a trailblazer. Give it a new job: the task of looking out for opportunities rather than threats or dangers.

If you tend to be skeptical and are always on the lookout for when you are going to get scammed, your distrustfulness and doubts may stop you from taking action. However, those same qualities also mean you are able to see down the road, to see the big picture. You are a strategist. The work, then, is to use those qualities in a positive way instead of letting them stop you.

In truth, a setback or a breakdown is only a test of your commitment to your vision. View them as challenges, and reconnect to your Big Why. Remember your motivation for being a successful entrepreneur in the first place.

When you view setbacks as challenges, they don't knock you down. You just find a new way forward. You emerge victorious.

How Do You See the World?

Your life is like a movie, and the person sitting next to you or in the other room is viewing a very different movie. The director of your movie is your perception. The way you experience anything and everything comes from how you perceive it. Is a setback a challenge or a catastrophe? It depends on how you view it. The way you view a setback is determined by your experiences, the meanings you ascribed to them, and the beliefs you created from them.

What if setbacks are only illusions, similar to the distractions that occur when people compete? Not only can you change the way you view setbacks, but you can also change the lens of your perception. You can change the way you see *anything*. We are going to start with beliefs.

Beliefs Are Not Always Based on Logic

Beliefs are powerful. They determine whether or not you are going to be a go-getter. Consider the unknowns who became exceptional industry leaders despite the odds against them. They believed they were capable of great results, and they were. However, there are many more entrepreneurs who possessed the technical ability to make an impact but didn't believe they were capable. Their stories are rarely told.

Basically, a belief is the relationship between a thought and an emotion. As we grow up, situations and people influence us. Things happen in our lives that have emotional impacts. We create meanings around them and then form beliefs based on those meanings.

There is a difference between belief and reality. Beliefs are not always based on facts or logic, although they can feel very true. Beliefs, however, shape your reality.

Many of our beliefs were formed when we were very young, prior to age seven. This is an important fact. Before age seven, you were unable to distinguish between reality and fiction. Remember when you believed in the

Tooth Fairy, the Easter Bunny, and Santa Claus? Many of your beliefs were created in those formative early years then got tucked away into your subconscious mind.

As you grew up, you continued to create other beliefs, which also eventually went underground, becoming subconscious. You might not be aware of those beliefs, but they guide each decision you make and every action you take.

Over your lifetime, you have formed a variety of beliefs about your self-worth, abilities, and goals, and many of them have worked to your advantage. Other beliefs, however, prevent you from challenging the status quo. This is neither good nor bad; there is no judgment. Everyone possesses beliefs about their abilities.

Some of those beliefs are conscious and some are subconscious, or hidden. An example of a conscious belief is, *I deserve success*. A subconscious belief I had to contend with early on was, *I have to do it all myself.*

Subconscious beliefs are always more powerful than conscious beliefs, in part because they operate under the surface and we usually don't know they are there—but they still direct our actions. In fact, if you have two opposing beliefs, one conscious and the other subconscious, the subconscious belief will always dominate.

How often do you see an entrepreneur who wants more clients but whose income never goes beyond a specific amount? Something in that person's subconscious mind feels threatened about money and success. It is as though they possess a speedometer on cruise control concerning the cost of success and wealth. If they try to aim too high or too low, the speedometer self-corrects to its set point.

Did that hit home? I bet it did. Most of us have something similar. I worked with a photographer who said she always earned about four thousand dollars per month. Periodically, her monthly income would rise to five thousand, or even six thousand, but not consistently. Her perception about earning four thousand dollars per month was setting her average. We reset the cruise control on her speedometer to allow for greater income, and she began having more months that generated six thousand dollars per month, which improved her annual income.

Conscious and subconscious beliefs are often in opposition to one another. Many subconscious beliefs are based on situations that don't exist anymore, and they were usually founded on incomplete information to begin with. For instance, if your parents got divorced soon after you got in trouble for hitting the dog, you might conclude that the divorce was your fault. You couldn't know the complexity of your parents' relationship; you only knew that you were "bad," and then Daddy left. You did not have all of the information, but in order to make sense of the situation, you developed your own meaning to explain what happened.

You completed a puzzle without all the pieces. You created a picture, but it wasn't accurate. Still, you formed a belief in your "badness," which moved into your subconscious mind and now creates problems for you when it gets activated or opposes a conscious belief.

Two opposing beliefs, especially a conscious and a subconscious belief, create conflict and an inner struggle. For example, you might say you are committed to being a successful business owner, but if you subconsciously believe you don't deserve it or don't want the attention, you will hold yourself back, or worse yet, sabotage your success. Or you may become a perfectionist, slowing down your progress to avoid being judged for making a mistake.

Inner struggles are draining. Trying to think them through or tough them out will not help, because the struggle is not based on logic. It is energetic. It is like a water hose with a kink in it. No matter how far you turn the faucet, the water will not flow. The kink holds back the water, creating pressure in the hose. Once you take the kink out, the water flows freely.

When you develop an inner struggle because of two opposing beliefs, your energy has a kink in it, and progress becomes very difficult. Clear the kink, and you begin to progress once more.

How to Clear the Kink

My client Allan was a nationally acclaimed online marketer who was on the verge of burnout. He was very happy with his income, but setting boundaries was not easy for him. Although he has great technical abilities, he was stretched too thin. He told me he was not taking charge of his business, so he was now doing unfulfilling jobs. He talked about the challenges of dealing with critical clients, how tough it was to set boundaries, and how he blamed himself for missing deadlines.

His language was all about struggle, which told me he had an internal struggle, a collision between conscious and subconscious beliefs. When I pointed this out to him, he was willing to explore his hidden beliefs and make connections between those beliefs and his current results.

After some discussion, he admitted his work had turned into a grind. Dealing with critical clients was draining. He worked long hours, his wife was always talking about him never being available, and as he continued to avoid difficult conversations, he felt the pressure of more and more being expected from him.

Like a lot of entrepreneurs, he had the common belief that he needed to tough it out. Yes, that is one way to avoid difficult and unfulfilling circumstances. It is not, however, the easiest way, nor is it going to achieve the quickest, longest lasting results. It certainly wasn't working for Allan.

Allan's solution was much simpler. Rather than tough it out, I suggested he put into action a new belief that he could restructure his business according to his ideals. I suggested he fire his unappreciative, critical clients so he would feel more capable, and to find ways to bring the fun back into his life again. I told him if he shifted his focus to the projects he enjoyed most and not procrastinate with busy work, he would get more done and be more focused.

He agreed to consider those suggestions, with the goal of enjoying his work and cutting back on the long hours. To really make this work, however, his wife needed to be aware of the plan. She agreed to stop talking about the work-life imbalance and vowed to be more supportive.

With his new belief that he could take charge of his business and the support from his wife, Allan eventually fired his non-ideal clients and became excited about the new direction of his business.

Some beliefs are easily changed on your own once you recognize them. Others are more challenging. They can be changed but are more deeply rooted. Once you are genuinely ready to replace your beliefs with something new and relevant, it will happen. Change is possible.

An Exercise to Clear the Kink

To begin to clear your own kink caused by conflicting beliefs, try the same three-prong approach I used with Allan:

1. Uncover the hidden beliefs affecting your actions. First, examine your resistance. Where are you not excelling as expected? When do you hold yourself back? When do you make excuses, blame others, or feel fear? In those situations, you are likely experiencing conflicting beliefs. Choose one situation and try to find the belief that is informing your action or inaction. (To do this, you might need the assistance of a therapist or business coach.)

2. Discover the relationship between the belief and the consequences it is having on your actions. The easiest way to do this is to become aware of the thoughts you have as you are doing different activities. How do those thoughts influence your actions? After you complete a specific activity, write down where you experienced flow and what was occurring. Also note when you felt that remaining focused was difficult and what was going on then.

3. Regain control by exploring alternative beliefs better suited for your current reality, and put those beliefs into action. The ideal time to do this is at the end of the day, when you have time to reflect on your activities.

If you have difficulty with this exercise, don't despair. Sometimes, it takes a trained professional to help you clear the obstacles to success. As it is with mentoring, transforming the obstacles will occur at a faster pace when you work with someone else than when you work on them on your own.

The Power of Your Story

The beliefs you have feel true, but they are creations of your experiences. They stem from your interpretations of the things that happen to you and the stories you tell yourself in order to make sense of the events.

We all have a story, and each of our stories is unique. Our stories can inspire us or hold us back. You will learn how even the ones that hold you back can be transformed.

Lisa, a client and pediatric nutritionist, is preparing to expand her clinic. During a session, we were talking about her childhood as the oldest of five children and how she grew up too quickly. She helped care for her younger siblings and missed out on a carefree childhood.

Lisa was expected to help her mom with chores and watch the other kids. She told me that her parents never asked her what she wanted. They called her "little mama" and teased her about being perfect. Instead of her parents caring for her, she cared for her parents.

Lisa's home life was chaotic. Coming home from school was nerve-wracking, since she never knew what was on the other side of the front door. She craved order, so she created rules to help her make sense of her world. Lisa believed that she had to do everything herself and never learned to ask for help.

Lisa endured this situation all through school, and it eroded her confidence. When you hear something repeatedly, you begin to believe it. When Lisa came to me, she admitted she did not like disorganization and would rather know exactly what to expect, which posed a problem for her. When unexpected challenges arose and her staff didn't follow through as expected, she picked up the slack. You can imagine how her control issues would create an inner struggle and slow down her growth plan.

How We Changed Lisa's Story to Match Her Goals

Most people never stop to examine their beliefs to see if they ought to be updated. Then when something occurs in the present to activate one of those subconscious beliefs you formed when you were a child, you respond or react to it like a child without even realizing it.

It is as though your five-year-old self steps up and starts driving the bus. Now, five-year-olds do not have the skill set or maturity to drive responsibly—you don't want them directing your responses. Yet, when a triggering event occurs, we may respond from a very old place, especially when caught off guard. That is why you see entrepreneurs over-think choices and decisions that appear risky.

Luckily, humans are extremely adaptable. Our brains have plasticity, which is one of the reasons we have survived as a species. We are flexible, evolving beings. And we can use our innate adaptability to change our future and even how we think of our past.

Just as you can change how you view setbacks, you can change how you view your memories. When you do that, you don't have to forget the memory, you just alter how you look at it and the way it affects you. Ideally, the memory loses its charge, its emotional intensity. Once that is gone, you are free to create a new response to a situation that previously would have triggered a reactive response.

Rather than perceiving an event the way the five-year-old you viewed it and believing the story that was created, you get to rewrite the story and perceive the event from an adult's point of view. This impacts your decisions, your business, and your life.

We changed Lisa's story around her childhood experience of growing up too quickly in only one session. Using EFT and visualization, we shifted her focus from the negative, being teased as "little mama," to the positive.

Using visualization, I took Lisa back to a memory of cooking dinner and had her see herself there as the young girl she was and also as the woman she is today. Most of the emotional charge around that incident was anger at her mother for not taking care of her, so while I did the EFT, I invited her to say all the things to her mother that she had wanted to say for two decades. This caused a big emotional release for her.

We then created a new mind movie, altering the memory to be positive by reframing her days spent caring for her younger brothers and sisters as a major contributor to her vow to nourish children. She transformed a lifelong negative memory into a strong motivator for becoming a leading pediatric nutritionist. By doing so, she reconnected to her personal commitment to teach children how to have a healthy life and that they matter.

Instead of holding on to a negative memory that her needs didn't matter, which held her back, Lisa now sees how her own childhood influenced her choice to help children learn healthy habits. In addition, we developed a powerful visualization of her being a successful leader in her field that she can now tap into.

Changing Lisa's story significantly boosted her confidence to expand her clinic. She now knows how to remain focused and dismisses things that would have previously disrupted her sense of order. After one session, her response to unexpected challenges improved significantly.

Retool Your Inner Critic

A relentless inner critic can cause a kink that prevents you from thinking like a leader. Most top entrepreneurs have very high standards for themselves. They feel they never perform to their best capabilities, that there is always something they could do to push their limit a bit more. Those thoughts of always wanting to do more and never being satisfied can, and do, motivate a person to try harder and to work harder.

At a certain point, however, self-criticism can backfire. Those thoughts of never doing well enough are very negative, and negativity slows down progress. For instance, when you are critical of yourself, you tend to second-guess everything you do, causing you to hold back, fearful of making a mistake and being criticized again, if only by yourself. And giving so much energy to what you are not doing well drains you. It is exhausting.

Change is difficult when you are focused on what you don't want to do, what is not working for you, and what you are not doing well. When you keep looking behind you, you are going against the flow and hindering your success. Remember, whatever you focus on expands.

When you think negative thoughts, you will always find evidence to support your reality. It is like rafting upstream on a river. By going against the current, you spend a lot of energy resisting the river's natural flow. It is tiring and exhausting. For the amount of effort you are exerting, you have little gain in return. On the other hand, when you turn your raft around to go downstream with the natural current of the river, it flows easily with little effort.

In the same way, when you turn your attention toward what *is* working, what you *are* doing well, and where your business is improving, you are looking forward. You are positive and hopeful, excited by what is possible. Your raft is now going downstream, aided by the current. You begin taking steps toward reaching your full potential.

It is important, however, to be aware of the messages your critical voice is telling you. If you are not aware of them, you cannot change the situation. Some entrepreneurs are not aware, so they are attacked and don't even know it. As a result, they may act out, underachieve, or be unpredictable or moody.

How to Become Aware of the Inner Critic

If you are not aware of the self-critical voice in your head, it is possible to learn to hear it. Just as you keep records on your business cash flow, you can keep a log or journal on the thoughts you have that create distraction for you. You can also keep a log of thoughts that create laser focus. You might be surprised to find that when you are laser focused, your mind is clear and free of all thought. When you begin to log your thoughts, you start to bring something that was subconscious up to the surface. Once you are aware of those hidden thoughts, you can begin to change the situation.

Next, it is important to understand how those negative thoughts affect your performance. As you are writing in your log, record the connections between thoughts and a specific result. For instance, you are a graphic designer, and you recall that you were beating yourself up for taking an unexpected call while working on a project that was due the next day and, as a result, you lost focus. This is the connection between the thought (beating yourself up) and its result (losing focus).

Once you become aware of the self-critical messages, the trick is to not believe them. They sound justified, but they are not. They originally came from someone else, perhaps a parent or teacher. Most likely you heard them from someone you wanted praise from but never got. You can choose to transform your inner critic, and as you do, you are freeing yourself of the negative drag on your actions.

An Exercise to Sidestep Your Inner Critic

Here are six steps for transforming your relationship with the inner critic:

1. First, understand that the inner critic is fearful. Fearful thoughts can easily take on a life of their

own, causing a complete halt of any progress if ignored. What are the fears that keep you stuck?

2. You get to choose how you view your progress and performance. Despite what your inner critic says, you don't have to focus on the negative, on what you are not doing well, in order to excel. Remember, to do so is like rafting upstream. Create a strengths-based approach, finding the positive activities that help you improve.

3. You may feel as though the inner critic is part of you, but it is not. Being aware of this will help you separate from the critical voice. Where did the critical thoughts originate? If you hear them, do you recognize the voice?

4. Once you recognize you have a choice to release the inner critic, you have created your opportunity for change. Choose not to believe the voice anymore.

5. Your goal is not to annihilate the voice; your goal is to make it irrelevant. Do that by shifting your focus to the positive. Acknowledge the activities you are doing well. Become aware of your strengths. Choose the next step toward your vision. Think about your goals.

6. Notice the results. As you begin changing your perception and thinking like a growth-minded entrepreneur, the resistance to your excellence collapses, and you will start to see improvement in your actions. In addition, you will have a much-improved state of mind.

To be a successful entrepreneur, you have to think like a successful entrepreneur, see yourself as a successful entrepreneur, and act like a successful entrepreneur. Each of these steps is more involved than it seems on the surface.

As with Lisa, you must be willing to delve into memories you wish you could forget. The good news is that once you do, you are free. You will no longer have a drag on your actions. You will have fewer distractions affecting your focus, and your effectiveness will certainly improve.

You can choose to release yourself from the struggle, your resistance, and your inner critic. Thinking like a successful entrepreneur changes your brain chemistry and sets the stage for an upward spiral and a breakthrough in your actions. I know that is what you want, so let's continue.

3: Successful Entrepreneurs Think Outside the Box

A business owner's odds for success increase with time. Fifty percent of all small businesses will survive the first five years, and it is possible to tip the odds for success in your favor.

Highly successful entrepreneurs, similar to champion athletes, pursue a vision. The desire to succeed is greater than any concerns of failure. They are not afraid to pursue something and risk failure.

Deeply motivated entrepreneurs go the extra mile, pushing themselves in ways most entrepreneurs don't. For example, Alli Webb, the founder of Drybar, pursued her vision even though she was a stay-at-home mom.

As a six-year-old, she had super-curly hair and would beg her mother to straighten it with the blow dryer. Her self-confidence rose when her mom styled her frizzy hair.

Webb started her business by driving to women's homes with her blow dryer in hand, and her hairstyling appointments revolved around her baby's play dates and nap times.

She realized women would pay as much as forty dollars for an expert blow dry. No cuts, no color on the menu like other salons. Instead, she pictured a beautiful space with a fun atmosphere to get a fantastic blowout. With the financial support of her brother, Webb opened the first Drybar in 2009. In seven years, her business evolved from driving to each client's home to growing a multi-million-dollar company.

Instead of waiting for someone to tell them what to do, motivated entrepreneurs take a proactive role with their business, including seeking support in areas that are not their personal strengths.

A client who is an accountant realizes that he has a tendency to be too much in his head. While restructuring his business, he wasn't sure how to raise his rates. I asked him whose business model inspired him, which encouraged him to shift from hourly billing to value-based pricing. He has a role model who had already made this transition, so he reached out to this person, attended seminars on the topic, and developed his new service and pricing plan. Instead of complaining about trying to increase his income and being frustrated, he took a proactive role and got the training he needed.

As a result, he paid off outstanding business debt two years earlier than scheduled. He dreamed of one day buying the building where his business is located and is now negotiating that purchase. These two opportunities never would have occurred so quickly if he continued to remain with the status quo.

Be Open to Unusual Opportunities

Success-minded entrepreneurs look for opportunities to help them reach their goals, and those opportunities might not be usual and customary. In fact, to be a highly successful entrepreneur *requires* out-of-the-box thinking and a more creative approach.

A traditional in-the-box business model is what most entrepreneurs are doing. In this model, you go with the flow, don't question things, and accept the feedback you get as fact instead of considering that there might be a better way. If your intention is to remain average, then this approach will serve its purpose. Entrepreneurs who desire continued growth ought to modify traditional practices and create a business blueprint tailored to their vision. Make note of the particular areas in your business where your clients get exceptional results, then consider modifying your business model to optimize those areas. Business excellence requires commitment and perseverance.

If you want to be a successful entrepreneur, you have to rise above the rest. If you just do what everybody else is doing, you will get the same results they do. If you want different results, you have to differentiate yourself from the competition. Below are a few ways to begin.

How to Break Out of the Box

Push the edge. You do have to learn the rules first, but once you understand them, you can break them, go beyond the theory, and push the edge. Business owners who arc geared for success are compelled to look for new ways forward. They want to discover how to deliver a fantastic service and be profitable.

Be open to inspiration, no matter where it originates. As it did for my accountant client, your inspiration might come from a role model in your own industry, or it might come from a different profession altogether. You may take a concept from bookkeeping and apply it to photography, for example.

I do this all the time when I apply sports and success concepts to business growth, which, in fact, transfer very well. For example, the three components necessary for success are the same for both sports and business growth: have a vision of what you want to be; have the motivation to keep going and staying connected to your vision, even when obstacles arise; and take action to continue moving toward your vision.

Similarly, you might study highly successful people in other industries to determine whether what they did to achieve their success will transfer to your profession. Inspiration is all around you. You have only to be open to it.

View failure differently. You have to stop seeing failure as negative. Instead, view it as a learning opportunity that highlights the areas that need further strengthening or shows you where a new approach might be necessary to reach your desired results.

Connect with entrepreneurs who are like-minded. If you are a highly driven entrepreneur, it is important to connect with other highly driven entrepreneurs, inside and outside of your profession, because they know things you don't know yet, and vice versa. Just as 1+1=3, the two of you coming together form a third consciousness, out of which can develop new ideas and inspiration.

Take personal responsibility. Instead of relying on someone to tell you what to do and then just following that person's direction, take ownership of your vision and goal. Ask questions and seek information to help you get where you want to go.

If your current mentor is able to take you to a particular point in your career but no further, look for the person who can stretch you to reach your goal. Or, if your current mentor is not the best match for you—perhaps he or she is high strung or overly negative—and you are in a position to choose your mentor, find the person who is going to support you in the way that works best for you.

However, if you *can't* find a coach or mentor, don't complain about it or throw in the towel; find someone else who can give you the support you need. Perhaps an associate is seeking an accountability partner and her temperament is an ideal match for you.

But before you give up on your first mentor, if your mentor is approachable, communicate your needs to him or her. I know, some aren't approachable, but some are if you approach them with respect. Take the initiative to educate your mentor about your best learning style.

You have yet another option. If you don't like the way your mentor communicates with you, try to look past the negativity and really understand the mentor's intention. Your mentor wants you to do well because when you do well, he or she looks good. Learn how to perceive differently what your mentor, or even your employees, are saying. A lot of times, you can change your perception, and your experience, simply by not taking feedback so personally, even though it feels personal. You can make a decision to not get upset anymore.

Look for the Purple Cow. As Seth Godin wrote in his book *The Purple Cow*, when you are driving along the highway and you see all the black-and-white cows, you don't really take any notice because they blend in with the expected scenery. However, if all of a sudden you see a purple cow, you are going to stop, pull your car over, and really look at the cow because it is different.

If you are looking to change things in your industry, traditional methods are not going to get you there. You need to look for a different approach. You need to look for the purple cow.

A current example of this is companies that test driverless cars. They are positioning themselves to disrupt the entire transportation industry. Uber set out to challenge the car-for-hire industry, and Travis Kalanick, CEO of Uber, continues to challenge industry norms. He started testing driverless cars in Pittsburgh, Pennsylvania, and as a result, he is now expanding his pilot test program to California. Uber claims that eventually the entire fleet will use autonomous vehicles. The plan is to rapidly replace their one million-plus human drivers with robot drivers.

Uber is dedicated to aggressively updating their fleet. The combination of surrounding himself with the greatest minds and having an aggressive pilot program are the perfect combination. Kalanick found the purple cow. He is moving forward and challenging the status quo to adapt or get out of the game.

Yes, other companies have successfully disrupted "how things have always been." Advancing technology continues to open doors by combining an idea with a vision that creates a shift. From there it is a matter of advancing and waiting for the rest of the world to catch up.

What separates Uber from Google's and Tesla's autonomous driving programs is the end result. Basically, the other companies want to build and sell their driverless vehicles. Uber has no interest in developing the technology to build the vehicles. Kalanick's aim is to partner with companies who can supply the cars and then replace his fleet.

Remember, success is 90 percent mindset. Entrepreneurs who step up with confidence, believe in their vision, and advance their business in a manner different from entrepreneurs who think solely about how to compete in their marketplace will be the highly successful ones.

Vision-Based, Out-of-the-Box Actions

Don't misunderstand me—there are definitely aspects of the traditional business model you ought to be doing because they have been proven to work. My point is, don't stop there. Look for opportunities that will help you reach your vision regardless of where the opportunities come from.

At first, these opportunities might not appear to make sense or might seem inconvenient, but be receptive to them, because in the long run, they will help you get where you want to go at a quicker pace.

A powerful example of out-of-the-box thinking occurred in the vacation rental market. People need a place to stay when traveling, and booking rooms is easily accomplished thanks to technology. But now, local, privately owned bed and breakfasts are lagging behind Airbnb.

As Airbnb accommodations began dominating the local market, they created a new challenge for higher priced traditional bed and breakfast accommodations. Was there a solution? A small, quickly growing online reservation service for bed and breakfast accommodations emerged. This company cracked the code on how to turn B&Bs into highly profitable properties with the booking sites already used by travelers.

This reservation system integrates all of the online booking sites into one calendar. One property is listed on multiple sites, and the listing is automatically updated and removed from all online sites once it has been booked. The entire process is automated.

This service helped accommodation owners fill their rooms, even during low seasons. Properties that were barely surviving are now highly profitable. The founder for this business applied concepts he already knew to create a program that fit his vision of sold-out properties for inn keepers.

In another example closer to home, I was working with an inventor who created a product that eliminated mold and fungus with a non-toxic, organic formula. This product eliminated the need for toxic pesticides and herbicides, and the farmers who used it on their crops reported healthier plants. Harvest yields were significantly increased because the product reduced the number of unhealthy plants that a grower needed to destroy. But the government required cost-prohibitive testing and certifications before the inventor could sell his product on the market.

An unlikely solution arose when a house restoration company accidently discovered that the product eliminated black mold. Restoring homes didn't have as many bureaucratic barriers, and with the help of a research and development department, the product was safety tested for use in homes and work places without the toxic side effects of traditional formulas. This is a perfect example of thinking outside the box.

Learn to Love What Challenges You Today

I encourage you to love the challenges you currently face. Isolate the circumstances of your biggest challenge, then develop the skills to effectively overcome it.

For example, some entrepreneurs don't like sales conversations because they don't like to directly ask for payment. For those entrepreneurs, closing the sale is very frustrating. They are aware of their own discomfort and the potential client's response when asked to sign up and pay. This part of the consultation drains their energy and shifts focus away from the potential client. Instead of being focused on helping a potential client, they become distracted by their own ill ease about money and avoiding disappointment.

If I have just described you—you don't like getting to the end of a consult, when it is time to close the sale— then practice those conversations so you can learn how to remain focused on your potential client throughout the entire process and even find out how to love those conversations.

When you learn to love what you have always hated or avoided, you will have a very different outlook. Sales conversations will be just another way to challenge yourself. Or you might be neutral and think, *Okay, this is not my favorite part of the consultation, but hey, I'm here. I'm going to do my best to help this person.* This will have a very different effect on your focus and actions than if you get upset, frustrated, and flustered about something that is a necessary part of owning a business.

If you think learning to love something you currently hate is not possible, let me tell you, it is. For twelve years I avoided asking for help and worked independently in our satellite office. My preference was to offer my clients an experience that surpassed industry standards. I wanted to "wow" them. While I enjoyed working with my clients in our counseling agency, I was a lone wolf who kept tight control over my case load. My control issues interfered with our agency's growth.

Working with other therapists who excelled at either the paperwork or client services, but rarely both, was torturous. I knew I had to get past my aversion to get help, so I tackled the issue and *got out of the way* of supervising other clinicians. I pushed past my control issues and was happy to pass on non-ideal clients.

Allowing others to assist me offers more opportunity than doing it all myself. Working side by side with other therapists offered challenges, but it also opened new opportunities. Our agency grew. Working with a support staff frees up my time to focus on the things I do best: helping my clients get out of their own way to achieve their full potential. I now actually prefer to pass over work that is necessary but that I don't enjoy.

To make a similar shift for yourself, understand that you are not given any challenges you are unable to overcome. If you connect with your vision and you can see yourself having reached your goal, then the way for you to attain it is always available to you.

You will have to move outside of your comfort zone, and as explained in chapter 2, reframe any beliefs holding you back. For instance, I believed other therapists wouldn't maintain the same level of service for our clients, but once I gave it a chance, I saw that my belief wasn't true. The action didn't change; I still needed another therapist to work alongside me. But how I perceived the situation had changed, and that changed everything.

Part Two:
See Yourself Enjoying Success Now

4: Where Is Your Focus?

*Focus 90 percent of your
time on solutions and only
10 percent of your time on
problems.*

— Anthony J. D'Angelo

You Are a Star

Everything you need in order to succeed is available to you right now. All you need to do for your dream to become a reality is to believe it is possible and then take action when the opportunities appear. It really is that simple.

Now, this does not mean that all you have to do is think about something and it will happen, and it doesn't mean you won't face setbacks along the way. What it does mean is you need to recognize and say yes to the opportunities that are available to you right now.

For instance, what could you be doing to improve your business right now? Would you benefit by working with a marketing agency, sales person, or business coach? Could you enhance your customer experience or service delivery model? Explore different ways to fulfill a client need?

Growth-minded entrepreneurs are committed to excellence. They adopt a no-excuses approach to their business and how they serve their clients. Commit now to strive for excellence. Look for the next step that can take you to your goal, then follow through and take action.

The Brick Wall

Along the way to your goal, you will be tested to see how committed you are to excellence. Remember what I wrote about setbacks? Napoleon Hill, the author of *Think and Grow Rich*, called setbacks the "sly guises of opportunity." They appear unfortunate, but they are not. These moments separate highly successful entrepreneurs from the rest.

For example, as your business grows and gets busier along the way, eventually you will plateau, and your progress will come to a halt. You will experience a sales slump. A setback. You will hit a brick wall.

Most entrepreneurs respond to a brick wall by digging in, trying harder, and doing whatever they can to get past it. As with competitive people, when driven entrepreneurs are confronted with the fight, flight, or freeze response, they want to fight. White-knuckling and working through it feels like the natural response.

The problem is that trying to force the situation actually creates more of a struggle, because you get very focused on what is not going well, which can dig you in deeper. Think of the quicksand analogy—if you step into quicksand, the more you fight and struggle, the quicker you will sink. The best response to quicksand is to relax, which actually buys you time to look around for the opportunity to get yourself out.

The same is true when you are in a sales slump or plateau. Instead of struggling and digging yourself in deeper, take some time to assess the situation. View the brick wall as a test to see how committed you are to your vision. Also, realize that a plateau is an indicator that you are on the verge of a breakthrough. Check that your actions are aligned with your intentions, that what you say you want and what you are doing are complementary. This sets up your business to achieve the next level of success. It appears at first to be a setback, but it is not. Rather, it is an opportunity to correct any actions that contradict your core values. Getting your thoughts in sync with your actions will successfully prepare you for the next level of success.

This is similar to the way you harness your energy right before you launch a new product, host an event, or gain a big new account: you wait for the important moment to arrive, and you anticipate your turn. Think about the physical and mental experience, the way you buzz with energy right before you "go."

Your slump or setback is the same. Transition periods *require* larger amounts of focused effort to allow you to successfully leap from where your business is now to where you want it to be. In truth, this is happening all the time, but when it appears unexpectedly, it catches you off guard and throws everything off balance.

Instead of getting discouraged, keep your faith and remain connected to your vision of what you can control right now. Continue to work in your business and on advancing your business, whatever you need to do, but remain confident that your business will continue to grow.

The Most Success Entrepreneurs Value Progress and Learning

When highly successful entrepreneurs smack into a brick wall, they keep their focus on where they want to go and continue to take the necessary steps to regain momentum. They look for any opportunity to get where they want their business to go. Their vision is clear, and they are committed to taking quick, decisive action while maintaining their focus on their goal.

They are also more committed to progress than perfection. This is important, and it is a departure from traditional thought. More often than not, entrepreneurs are concerned about their image and avoid mistakes at all costs. Well, what if avoiding mistakes turned out to be costly? What if it cost priceless insights? Would you become less concerned with appearances and more committed to making the attempts?

If a highly successful entrepreneur's action is not perfect, he or she will make adjustments along the way. A success mindset puts the ego aside and values experience over appearance. Failure is not an option. Instead, the business owner views mistakes as learning opportunities, and corrections and adjustments as steps on the path to excellence.

Entrepreneurs who have hit a brick wall are weighted down in some capacity. Something old needs to be let go in order to move forward. It is like being the pilot of a hot air balloon who wants the balloon to go higher, to a new altitude. To achieve that new height, the balloon needs to lighten its load. Perhaps you need to do the same. What do you need to let go?

When you look at the statistics, highly successful entrepreneurs actually have more setbacks than others. They also put more time into their personal development than everyone else, stretching themselves, testing new approaches, and pushing toward the edge. These entrepreneurs are set on what they believe is possible, even when others have doubt. "No" is not an acceptable answer for driven entrepreneurs. Instead of stating they can't do something, they wonder how they can make it happen.

For example, Richard Branson is a daring entrepreneur who has launched more than four hundred companies. He dropped out of school at age sixteen to start his first business, *Student Magazine*. It never took off, so he jumped into a record mail order business. This business turned into his first store, Virgin Records. Virgin Cola was his most public failure. Branson admits that he "strayed from my own rules. Virgin only enters an industry when we think we can offer consumers something strikingly different that will disrupt the market. People were already getting a product that they liked, at a price they were happy to pay. Virgin Cola just wasn't different enough."

Branson believes in what his business is capable of achieving, and he refuses to allow mistakes, failure, or mishaps get him down. The results from following his personal philosophy speak for themselves.

Adopting a similar paradigm shift will begin to change your attitude and focus. It will get you ready for the breakthrough.

How to Get Beyond the Brick Wall

Getting beyond the brick wall does not mean you have to do it alone; you may need to find someone to help you make your leap to the next level of success. Successful entrepreneurs have a lot of support: mentors, consultants and strategic partnerships. The people who support you the most, believe in your ability to succeed, and share your vision of excellence want to help your business get beyond the brick wall. They want you and your business to succeed. They cannot do your work, but they continue to believe in your vision as you take the next step. They mirror your ability to achieve your vision.

As with Richard Branson, your commitment to your vision of what is possible propels you forward. Success comes from taking inspired action—seeing an opportunity and grabbing it. Success is a race against time on several dimensions. If you are working toward a specific goal, realize that the goal has also been seeded in other determined entrepreneurs. Many other entrepreneurs are dedicating their time, energy, and efforts to the very same outcome. So what one thing is necessary to declare success? The answer is *continued inspired action*. The industry leader takes inspired action toward his or her goal and then quick, decisive action. Implementing with speed separates the most successful entrepreneurs from the rest.

Where Do Your Eyes Land?

When you are growing your business, a myriad of distractions can disrupt your focus. These include disorganization, success envy, and unexpected interruptions that break your concentration. You could have some type of technical malfunction such as your online shopping cart going down during a new product launch, or perhaps your largest client didn't renew her contract or your trusted assistant gave notice or equipment malfunctions halted production and caused shipping delays.

You can also experience internal distractions, which are the thoughts and emotions you have in response to external distractions and any internal dialogue and thoughts about previous mishaps when you did not manage the situation effectively. You could be perceiving another entrepreneur as having more than you do, convinced that he is dominating the market or is more confident than you are.

These distractions shift your focus away from your plan and negatively affect your actions. Success envy impacts confidence. When you focus on the past, you may experience depression. When you focus on something you are afraid will happen, you will feel anxiety. Negative thoughts drain energy and cause self-doubt. Your inner critic slows you down.

Recently I was talking with a graphics designer who has been in the field for years. He knew what it felt like to be at a top ad agency and what he was capable of, but for whatever reason, he had hit a creative block.

He didn't understand why he was feeling stuck, and the tricks he knew to help him get centered and focused on design projects weren't working. He was struggling, blaming himself, and the situation was getting worse. His concentration was off, and his confidence was falling. Anxiety from his creative block grew as the deadlines approached. Because his unfinished work was constantly on his mind, he was bringing his work worries home. Being emotionally unavailable to his family led to tension at home.

The situation was also affecting his staff and the overall atmosphere in the office. He should have been leading his team but instead was avoiding all conversation. He was in a breakdown and knew he needed help.

If we were to work together, I could discover why he was so distracted, and then help him get out of the struggle. His new insight would help to rekindle his enthusiasm. I would also teach him the various mindset and focus techniques (visualization, EFT, and keywords) that I share in this book. Unfortunately, he will continue to struggle until he realizes a different path to take to unblock him.

Once a block has been identified and cleared, a void is created. This is why it is so important to replace something old with something new, to replace the negative with a positive.

I took this approach with an interior design client who came to me after being unable to shake the impact of a particular project where working with a highly critical client turned an easy room remodel into a nightmare. She was beating herself up about this client's criticisms, and it was affecting her confidence. Because she tends to be a perfectionist, she was looking at the job as a failure, and the incident was weakening her judgment and working against her.

I encouraged her to turn the situation around by viewing it as an opportunity to understand what was affecting her decisions in the first place, and then use the information to do something differently, thereby strengthening her overall composure.

This was also the approach the billionaire Mark Cuban took early in his career, fresh out of college. He was selling software and started out with little knowledge about computer software. He scheduled a hot sales call that conflicted with his obligation to open the store. Covering his bases, he asked a co-worker to open for him.

But when he returned to the store with a $15,000 check in hand from the early morning sale, his boss wasn't impressed. Cuban was fired on the spot. That was the pivotal moment when he decided that he was tired of working for someone else. His boss was his mentor, teaching him everything he didn't want to do as a business owner.

Rather than beat himself up for getting fired, he chose to look at the situation as an opportunity to launch his own business. He realized he wasn't suited to work as an employee. Cuban was more focused on getting the sale than worrying about not rocking the boat. By getting fired, he learned a valuable lesson that led to him starting his own company, MicroSolutions, and teaming up with Michael Dell.

Where Is Your Focus?

If you have had a disappointing client experience like the interior designer did, are you unable to get past it? Do your thoughts turn to failed jobs or unfavorable economic conditions? Are you easily distracted? Do you see a pattern here? All these thoughts are based on things you cannot control. You are spinning your wheels, wasting your most valuable asset—your energy—on something you have absolutely no control over.

Learning how to hone your focus and minimize the impact of distractions is vital. To do so, become aware of what your brain perceives as its object. For instance, do you tend to look at the end result you want to achieve or the outcome you want to avoid? If it is the latter, then the simple act of placing your focus on the desired result is your important first step. The next step is to learn to focus on what you want.

Focus Where You Want to Go

Thoughts, vision, and results are interconnected. If you believe something will happen, you begin to look for cues to affirm your belief. This creates conditions that eventually will produce an outcome supporting your belief. Simply put, if you believe something is true, it is. Everything will align itself to prove you are right. Your mindset is powerful. It can boost you up or bring you down.

One of my favorite things to do is to speak, both in person and virtually. I do this as frequently as possible, while focusing on delivering valuable information that can be quickly implemented.

Over the years, I have learned about the value of practice, practice, and more practice. Because of my commitment to improving my skill set, I have experienced some amazing outcomes.

Before a speaking engagement in 2014, I knew I would be presenting on the main stage to an audience of five hundred aspiring entrepreneurs. I was expected to deliver an engaging presentation, and this is where my mindset and focus became crucial.

I am constantly seeking to stretch beyond my current capabilities. Public speaking had been a long-standing fear, and speaking before an audience this size was stretching my comfort zone. You get the picture. How could I manage my nerves and deliver a dynamic presentation to the audience? Here is how.

Instead of being intimidated by the audience size, venue, and expectations, I stayed focused on my strengths, which are passion for my topic and maintaining laser focus. In order to deal with the waves of pre-performance anxiety, I knew focus techniques were necessary, and I was determined to maintain my composure.

I was the first speaker after the lunch break. The fifteen minutes prior to my time were brutal. While waiting in the Green Room, I did everything possible to manage my building anxiety. I reviewed my talking points, discussed final details with the event assistant, and remembered to breathe deeply to calm my nerves.

The emcee announced my name. I walked on stage and spoke from the heart. I put all I had into my presentation and felt connected to the audience. The anxiety melted away.

No one could have prepared me for the pre-performance anxiety. But *I* knew that dealing with the uncomfortable experience was an accomplishment, so I said yes to the speaking opportunity, although it made me nervous. My conviction, focus, and determination gave me the courage to challenge myself.

What it all boils down to is this: If you think you can do something, you can. If you believe you can't, you can't.

A realtor client learned this lesson recently. He was brokering a deal for a real estate investor client when complications arose with the sellers and the deal fell through. The investors switched to another realtor. In the past, losing an ideal client would have haunted him for days on end. Instead, rather than letting this failed transaction worry him and affect his work, he decided to learn from it, using several techniques I had taught him to gain insight and sharpen his skills. His result? What began as a disappointing failure turned into a milestone. He was awarded a top sales award!

Receiving this recognition was a game changer. He had been a local realtor for five years, and this sales award was an important marker. For several years he had come close, but not enough to be recognized as a top producer. He now knows what was once impossible is possible. He has increased confidence about his abilities and gets more respect from other agents.

If he hadn't had the mindset techniques, he likely would have allowed his failed transaction to throw off the rest of the year. He would have had a lot of negative inner dialogue and would have continued to chase his dream as a top producer, wondering if he could ever reach his goal. Instead, he kept his focus on the result he wanted and closed out his best year ever.

Frame What You Want in Positive Terms

Whatever you focus on expands, so if you are focusing on something you don't want to do or are worried about, then that very thing is likely to happen. This happens because, subconsciously, you are giving your brain messages to be attuned to the very action you don't want to have happen.

The brain operates through images. It doesn't have an image for the words "no" or "not." So when you think about what you *don't* want to happen—for instance, thinking "I do not want to mess up this deal"—the brain focuses on the noun and the verb, so it hears that you "want to mess up this deal."

This explains a lot, doesn't it? Just think about the videographer who is working with an important client and obsessing about all that could go wrong during the gig and hoping not to disappoint the client. Sure enough, she gets to the location, and she is so uptight that she rushes through the shoot and fails to do her best work. Or consider the aspiring sales professional who is in a sales slump. He is dwelling over the series of no's he has gotten while meeting with potential clients. He hopes he doesn't get rejected on this sales call but is worried that he will. He can't figure out what is going on. This happens because his brain wants to make him happy and does so by giving him what he is focused on.

Most of us are wired to focus on the negative, something that has been reinforced again and again since we were babies: *Don't do this. Don't touch that. Don't cross the street without looking both ways.* We don't even realize we are focusing on a goal or an objective from a negative point of view.

Another factor at play is that memory is reinforced by the amount of emotion we attribute to an experience. When we are focused on not messing up and then things don't go as planned, we get frustrated and angry and critical of ourselves. All of those emotions reinforce the memory.

In a psychology class I took, I was told about a medieval village that used strong emotion to pass down its oral history. On important days they wanted recorded, they would choose a young child and tell the child to really pay attention to everything that happened in the village that day. At the end of the day, they would take the child, who couldn't swim, and throw him into the water. They knew the fear he experienced would seal in his memories and the events of the day.

So ask yourself, What memories am I sealing in? Am I making sure I always remember my successes? Or am I perpetuating my disappointments?

If you are like most people, you are doing more of the latter, but it is possible to create a new habit. It is possible to begin focusing on the result you would like to have. Rather than saying you don't want to disappoint your important client, focus on what you do want to happen. If what you want is to create a two-minute video your client loves, envision yourself doing so before the day of your shoot. If you want to increase your percentage of closed sales, see yourself in your mind's eye calmly addressing the exact concerns your prospective client is sharing. Seeing yourself doing something is called visualization, a powerful tool we will explore in depth in chapter 6.

An Exercise to Train Your Inner Focus

With a crystal-clear inner focus, distractions lose their power to throw you off course, and you can remain steady under any and all conditions. Here is an exercise to help you develop your inner focus.

1. Develop a system to get the job done, and stick to it. Your plan is your blueprint. My preparation was crucial to me in dealing with my anxiety prior to my presentation. Some entrepreneurs either don't plan for things that could go wrong or throw the plan out the window because of self-doubt or to reduce pressure. It is okay to modify your plan according to unforeseen circumstances and in consultation, but don't second-guess it. Stick to the plan, based on your expertise, that you know works best.

2. After each project, evaluate your performance. Just as you track project management, keep track of your inner focus. Identify where and when you were able to maintain concentration. What were you doing when your focus was solid? Also log where and when you became distracted and whether it was from boredom, external factors, or thoughts in your head. What was happening at that point to affect your concentration? This exercise is similar to "An Exercise to Clear the Kink" in chapter 2. That exercise was related specifically to beliefs, whereas this one improves focus.

3. Learn and apply the lessons to the next project. Now look at your distractions. What can you learn about them? How could you have put things in place to avoid them? When you get into a similar situation, what could you do differently to maintain your focus? Where do you need to improve your focus in general, and what steps can you take for the next time you are in a similar situation? Prevention takes a lot less effort than intervention. Strengthening your focus requires discipline and effort, but it is absolutely worth it.

5: Stay Connected to Your Goal

Most entrepreneurs would agree that it is important to know what your specific success goal is. After all, without a definite milestone, you would never know when you had arrived.

Being able to state your clearly defined success goal and staying connected to it, however, are two different matters. When faced with a setback or breakdown, many entrepreneurs will disconnect from their vision and their goal because they don't recognize the process. They don't realize that if they work through the adversity, their breakthrough is right around the corner.

In fact, keeping your vision and goal really clear *enables* you to push through adversity and helps you keep your focus razor sharp. But too many entrepreneurs get so bogged down by what is going on for them, or they are beating themselves up so much, that their goal seems far away.

For instance, the bookselling chain Borders once dominated the book market, carrying tens of thousands of titles in a single store. The chain lost its edge in the mid-1990s, and because of technological advancements, Borders's market share dwindled. The chain responded by diversifying, adding CD and DVD departments as the industry shifted to digital. Borders mistakenly failed to develop a private label e-reader and instead handed over online sales to Amazon.

Borders's digital strategy aimed at getting buyers into the store. The way customers were consuming books had changed, but the company failed to accept that reality. They were stuck in a costly big box store model. These critical missteps led to the company filing for bankruptcy in 2011.

Another bookstore giant, Barnes & Noble, is a perfect example of a business who adapted to the changing market. Back in 2000, the company knew their online website was affecting in-store book sales. Their philosophy emphasized satisfying customer needs to maintain brand loyalty. This resulted in the company developing an online store and an e-reader to compete with Amazon and Kindle.

Rather than directing all spending to building store traffic, Barnes & Noble adapted to market demand for digital products. As of this writing, Barnes & Noble is still open for business. Amazon is the leading industry giant, yet industries that depend on Barnes & Noble are taking a wait-and-see attitude about whether they will survive.

Barnes & Noble didn't start out any different from Borders. The reason one survived while the other failed was foresight and risk. Barnes & Noble kept focused on how technology was impacting the book industry and trends in how people read books. They sought to adapt, and that is why they are still in business.

The Power of Congruency

If you want to stay connected to your goals and have the success you say you want, you also must have congruency, which is an alignment between your goals and your values, between what you present externally and how you feel on the inside. Lacking congruency is part of why entrepreneurs get stuck.

If you have any doubt about whether you are being congruent, look at your results. Are you taking all the steps you can to reach your goal, or do you freeze, remaining stuck? When there is incongruency between what you say you want and what you do, your actions give the clear picture of what is going on. Your internal beliefs and values drive you to either take action or remain inactive. Worse yet, having a disconnect between your values and goals contributes to sabotage.

For example, a dynamic health coach that I was working with has the natural talent and desire to help people beyond her local community. However, she wanted to help everyone instead of choosing a niche. Her desire to serve a wide audience actually limited her practice. Trying to reach all people kept potential clients from connecting with her and realizing she had the skill to help them regain their health.

At this point, she recognizes that her scope is too broad. She is concerned that if she chooses a specific niche, she may lose potential clients outside of that spectrum. That is entirely true. She is unable to know for sure if attempting to reach everyone has kept her from getting new clients until she chooses a niche clientele and focuses on their specific needs. Like many gifted entrepreneurs, she is strongly connected to her Big Why and possesses the passion inside herself to help people get back to feeling great once again. If she doesn't choose a niche, she will likely continue to struggle with attracting new clients.

Incongruency can also show up when entrepreneurs put all their focus on a single product that gets a disastrous response, and then hold back from quickly recovering because they fear another failure. There is a conflict between their goals and a value about safety that prevents them from quickly recovering from the loss.

Recently, I worked with a chef whose product caters to vegan diets. He had experienced a major setback when his largest client decided to part ways. The financial setback had him one late payment away from missing payroll. That one blow nearly collapsed his business. When he finally recovered from the setback, he recognized the need to diversify his clientele as a protective measure. He was spread too thin and reluctant to get help. As a result, he wasn't making up for lost business as quickly as he could have.

To help him refine his action plan in a way that would get results without draining his energy, we worked on his perception about the setback: his self-blame about putting his business in that situation to begin with, and the guilt he felt about letting several employees go because cash flow was tight. Before long, he was able to realign his values with his goals and begin again to put his business into overdrive.

How Do You Hold Yourself Back?

Many of us hold ourselves back for reasons other than
lack of diversification. We all have anxieties and things
we fear, and as a result, we avoid taking the necessary
action steps toward the things we say we want. We may
not even be aware we are doing it.

Some entrepreneurs secretly fear the added
responsibilities or increased expectations of others that
would come if they expanded their business, so they don't
take advantage of opportunities that could help them
grow. Others are afraid of letting people down. Still
others don't feel they deserve success, so when
opportunities arise, they might not take them.

If you are in a competitive profession, you may not
feel confident that you can do something that is contrary
to your industry, even though it would improve things for
your clients, so you stick with how things have always
been done. I have seen entrepreneurs second-guess
themselves before they even open their doors for business
when they think the competition is tough, more advanced,
and more experienced. They figure, *Who am I to do things
differently? I have no chance of ever getting that big,
anyway.*

I have seen entrepreneurs, particularly women, turn
down a leadership role because another business owner
wanted that position and they didn't want that person to
feel bad or didn't want to sacrifice a relationship with a
friend or didn't want to create conflict in a rivalry
situation, so they didn't lead when they could have. In
those instances, there is incongruence between their

actions, their underlying beliefs about how women should behave, and their values related to being "nice" or "not being bossy."

Sometimes entrepreneurs don't want to rise up and be more successful because of what they would have to give up. To be more successful, they might have to relinquish some privacy or time with their family, so their values of privacy and family collide with their business goals.

We have all had opportunities we haven't taken because we didn't feel we were experienced enough or prepared enough or had enough certificates hanging on our walls, awards of recognition on the mantel, or credentials after our names.

The trick is to bring awareness to what you are doing and not doing and why. We already explored ways to bring underlying beliefs to the surface. It is equally important to do the same with values.

If you have a value that contradicts your business goal, you will not move steadily toward your vision. Successful goals must be based on your values.

Are Your Values and Goals Congruent?

Simply put, values are things you care about. They tend to be the things we keep near and dear to our hearts. Many values will last a lifetime, and others will change according to professional and life circumstances. Your business is a value for you. Serving your clients is likely a value.

Since your values drive your actions and inaction, congruency between your values and goals is imperative. When they are congruent, your actions support your goals. For instance, I value earning income doing what I love, and I have the goal of being the best I can be for my clients. I support that value by the action of ongoing education, including continuing to work with my own business coach so that I continue to evolve along with my business. My value is congruent with my goal.

Because my bookkeeper client values his freedom, and his goal is to travel more, he has restructured from a brick-and-mortar business to a virtual bookkeeping practice. Those are actions he took to support his value of being able to work from anywhere, which is congruent with his goal.

An entrepreneur with a value of enjoying a certain lifestyle will support those values through the actions of maintaining client boundaries and managing her schedule so there is time for self-care. These actions would also support her goal.

When your values conflict with your goal, your actions will support your values but *not* your goal. Your subconscious mind is in a tug-of-war with your conscious mind. Being pulled in two different directions creates a struggle, and success is unlikely.

Sometimes we are not clear on what we really value, or we have outdated values we may not be aware of that are affecting our results. The good news is that values are fluid. Some will change as you change, but you can also take a proactive role. You can reframe your core values to be more appropriate for your present circumstances and goals. For instance, I did change my views about networking, but it took me several months to do so because I just couldn't see myself going to networking meetings. I valued my time, the introvert in me didn't want to speak before a large group of people, and the conversations always seemed superficial. In fact, I was having the experience of values colliding: the old one of avoiding loud social events and the newer one of growing my coaching business. Eventually, the desire to grow my business won out. I was fully committed to doing whatever was necessary to get known to the masses. That new value became so strong that I became willing to reframe the old one.

An Exercise to Discover Whether You Are Congruent

As you can see, congruency is key to your success. Determining what you actually value is vital so that you can decide consciously whether that value is working for you. This exercise, which is also available at http://BusinessSuccessSolution.com/book-bonus, will help you clarify your values and flush out any incongruencies that are getting in your way.

1. First, identify your core values. What do you care about? These could be your business, family, health, and so on.

_____

_____

_____

_____

_____

If you are having a hard time determining if something is a value, ask yourself these questions: Is it something I care about? Do I tell others that it is important to me? Do I support it with my actions? If you answer yes to these questions, it is probably a core value. We support the things we really care about with our actions.

2. Next, what are your goals?

_____

_____

_____

3. Do you see any obvious incongruencies between your values and your goals? If not, go on to the next question. If so, skip to number 5.

4. You want your actions to be complementary to your goals. Are the things you do on a daily basis supportive of your goal and the things you say you care about? If not, you probably have a conflict between a value and your

goal. Go back and study or add to your list of values until you see a incongruency. When you find it, go on to questions 5. If you have no incongruencies, congratulations! Your path to your goal should be clear.

5. It is time to re-examine your values and goals. Often, people have created values and goals for themselves based on what they think they "should" be doing or what someone else thinks is best for them. This approach might work for a while, but not for the long run. Spend some time to get really clear about what you care about and what you truly want to achieve. This is your life. Live it as you want to live it.

If you find that you have conflicting or outdated values, are you willing to update them? For example, when Tory Johnson, host of Good Morning America, worked for corporate America, she had someone else calling all the shots. When she was fired from a job she loved, she felt helpless about being let go for no cause. Then the recession rekindled her fear of being out of work and afraid.

At that time, she continued to work corporate jobs. However, the pink slip scar from corporate work was permanent. Her career goals began to change. She decided to be in charge of signing her own paycheck. With that seed planted in her mind, she put things in motion to go into business for herself. She realized her mission was to help women achieve their professional dreams.

Her career value to rise up the corporate ladder became incongruent with her new goal to take charge of her own success. Now she had a conflict—she had to choose between corporate employment and entrepreneurship. She chose to open her own business. She left corporate America behind, and now runs two successful businesses. She chose this for herself and her family.

Whether conscious or not, your values are the foundation for all your actions. Instead of going through life blindly and doing things just because that is how it is always done, take an active approach and choose the actions that are best for you. Generalizations don't work. Cookie cutter business models don't work, either. The more proactive and decisive you are, the better your results will be.

Further, when your values and beliefs align with your goals, your actions are in support of your goals, and seemingly magical opportunities present themselves. Only it is not magic, it is the power of congruency, and it is available to anyone who is willing to seek it.

6: See Yourself as a Success with EFT and Visualization

The significant problems we have cannot be solved at the same level of thinking with which we created them.

—Albert Einstein

Seeing yourself as a success is crucial because it creates the foundation on which to start making adjustments, even on a subconscious level, to your decisions and the direction you choose for your business.

Visualizing yourself as successful affects your approach to your business. You begin to step up with confidence, and this impacts your perception. Suddenly, the things you never considered doing become viable options.

When many entrepreneurs get started, their main focus is "to not fail," so they are likely to stay within their comfort zone and not take many risks. On the other hand, when you are focused on your vision, you will stretch beyond your comfort zone and go for opportunities you might have allowed to pass by if you were intent only on not failing. Also, the focus of "to not fail" is about avoidance, while achieving your vision is about flow, moving toward something, which is always easier than avoidance.

Entrepreneurs who are focused on not failing tend to be self-critical, whereas entrepreneurs who are committed to their vision tend to speak to themselves in a more positive way. Entrepreneurs trying to not fail tend to have an external locus of control and low self-confidence, and they need praise from other people to validate their worthiness. Entrepreneurs who are committed to their vision have a greater internal locus of control. They focus on actions that are within their ability to control, primarily attitude and execution. They self-coach.

The ability to self-coach is especially helpful when an entrepreneur doesn't have a direct connection to a business coach and a motivational, positive focus is desired.

Look Outside Your Comfort Zone

Most of us try to solve problems with the same thinking that caused the problems to begin with. People like staying within their comfort zone. Business owners, too, often try to solve business problems with the strategies they have always used.

The truly committed business owner is going to do whatever it takes to get results, and if there is an action that is a little bit out of the box, that is easy to apply and is effective and gets results, then not being open to doing it is a disservice to that business owner, her business, and her clients. I am talking about EFT, and I am challenging you to keep an open mind.

Why You May Need EFT

We often say things, do things, and set goals that directly contradict what we claim we really want. Often, we don't even know these contradictions exist, because they are below the surface. I addressed this earlier regarding underlying beliefs and values.

You might be highly committed to your goal and passionately want it, but if there is some subtle energy block around it, whether it is a thought, a belief, or how you view reality, you will have a struggle. You probably know entrepreneurs who do great when working directly with clients, but when it comes to marketing and sales, their actions are not up to par.

Being in that struggle is not necessary anymore. Your old way of thinking had you second-guessing yourself, avoiding the struggle, or over-thinking your way through it. But what if over-thinking isn't the solution? What if the problem is deeper, but also easier to shift because it has to do with energy? Think about how you feel energetically on a day when you are overwhelmed versus a day when everything is coming together. You feel focused and present on those great days. You feel wonderful, and everything is easy. There is no resistance. Your energy is flowing. Being in the zone is a timeless quality. It is almost as though you can slow down or speed up time.

EFT, or tapping, can help you make that shift. It can help you clear any conflict between what you say you want for yourself, where you are now, and where you want to be. It is also an incredibly simple technique you can learn and start using on yourself right away.

How EFT Works

Traditional business coaching focuses on actions and strategy. The underlying beliefs or emotions that affect your decisions are considered secondary. EFT, which stands for Emotional Freedom Techniques, works with acupressure points in the body to help neutralize negative emotions around a specific event and correct the flow of energy.

Think of a battery-operated flashlight. The batteries have a full charge, but if you put them in backward, the flashlight won't work no matter what you do, because the batteries are not making the right connection. However, when you turn the batteries around, a clean connection is created, and the flashlight works beautifully because the energy is flowing.

EFT works in much the same way. You tap with your fingertips on various acupressure points on your body as you focus on a particular emotional or physical issue, and balance is restored, often within minutes.

If you are skeptical, join the club. Remember, I was a skeptic, too, until EFT cured my life-long chocolate addiction.

EFT has been proven successful in thousands of clinical cases and is being adopted by many health care practitioners. It often works where nothing else will.

How Can EFT Help Me?

You may be wondering how EFT can help you succeed as an entrepreneur. Remember my client who was teased by her family and called "little mama?" After working with me and using EFT, she was able to distance herself from the memory that was holding her back. EFT didn't erase the memory or change the history of what actually happened, it disconnected the emotions attached to the event. After tapping, we used visualization to turn her responsibilities into a positive experience. As a result, the old memory, the actual one, lost its power over her.

The incident no longer has any emotional charge for her. She doesn't get triggered anymore. (A trigger is something that happens in the present that reminds you of a past pain, which causes you to react to the present incident as though it were the past pain. You think you are reacting to what is happening in the present, but you are not.) As a result of using EFT, my client is less reactive and more empowered. She can choose how she wants to act or react to any given situation that might formerly have been a trigger.

As a result of the original experience of being taunted as the caregiver for her family, my client had formed subconscious beliefs around her needs not being important and her view of herself as the peacekeeper. Through EFT, we were able to reframe the experience so that she doesn't respond from a childlike perspective to situations in which she feels like the peacekeeper. She created new beliefs about herself, who she is, and what she can do.

Another client, a general contractor, didn't win the bid on a large new construction project that would have opened doors to other contracts that size. He beat himself up about it and was very disappointed and self-critical.

We did EFT around him having been in a bidding situation where he had to compete against other established general contractors, about his feeling of disappointment, and of being a perfectionist and overly concerned about what people think of him. We were able to reduce the emotional intensity around all of those states. The next time he was asked to submit a proposal, he felt more confident and didn't experience the same anxieties. He remembers the disappointment from the previous time, but it doesn't haunt him anymore.

EFT has also been used to deal with money issues, which are related to anxiety and thoughts about money. Entrepreneurs experience tension regarding cash flow and pricing—it comes up over and over. EFT detaches entrepreneurs from their past associations with money issues and deals with the root of the anxiety. The next time they are in a similar situation, they don't have the same response. Their decisions are free of old beliefs regarding money, wealth, and self-worth.

What If?

Many people, whether they are business owners or not, live with the burden of *what if*. What if I took more risks? What if I pushed myself a little harder? What if I had had more confidence and followed through with that opportunity?

Early in her career, Oprah Winfrey was fired from a local news show because she was "unfit for television." What if she had believed that producer's statement and decided to call it quits? She would probably have had a very different outcome.

What if you don't try EFT and you can't get out of the struggle? What then?

Even though EFT appears to be unconventional and even weird, try it anyway. Be skeptical and try it anyway. If it doesn't work, you have lost nothing. But if it does work, you have found something very powerful.

The appendixes at the end of the book contain step-by-step instructions as well as samples you can model. If you want even more help, go to http://BusinessSuccessSolution.com/book-bonus for an opportunity to advance your business.

Take Your Visualizations to the Next Level

Many mindset mentors talk about visualization, a powerful tool for removing barriers and achieving one's full potential, and use it with their clients. Many entrepreneurs use it on their own, and they are probably getting results from it; however, most people do not experience visualization's full potential. Visualizing the way I teach in this book is like having a glimpse into the future, which you can then access whenever you want.

Visualization simply means imagining yourself achieving the best possible outcome in a given situation. You could call it a "mental dress rehearsal." Professional actors visualize their part in a production, repeatedly delivering a flawless performance in their mind's eye. It is a powerful training technique with a very real physical impact.

Visualization works in part because our minds are unable to discriminate between imagination and reality. This is why a dream can seem so real. Visualization creates new neuropathways in your brain in the same way the activity would if you were actually doing it. Repeatedly visualizing your success strengthens those pathways and contributes to actually attaining your goal. In addition, your subconscious mind will begin to look for opportunities to reinforce your visualized reality. You will begin to alter how you hold yourself, the way you respond to other people, and how you engage in your business. The change may be subtle, but over time, the shift in your behavior and identity will be substantial.

Top performers, regardless of profession, say they got started because they had a vision and then followed it. Olympic gold medalist Lindsey Vonn uses visualization prior to a competition. She gets quiet, and in her mind's eye, she sees herself skiing down the course. I am not privy to the details of her training, but she would be smart to use visualization while working on a new technique, as well. She could visualize herself using the new technique in order to speed her transition to it.

Fighter pilots rely on computer simulation programs when learning a new maneuver, and visualization is beginning to gain popularity as another tool to speed up their progress. Fighter pilots are not always able to rely on their eyesight, so visualization, in effect, becomes their eyes. By practicing a specific move thousands of times in their mind's eye, the move is already familiar when they are actually in the cockpit.

I was working with a social media marketer because she was having trouble with her sales conversations. I had her visualize the specific part of the meeting in which the room became silent after she shared her prices. She was able to see herself successfully remaining detached from her potential client's response. During a consultation two days later, she landed her first ten-thousand-dollar client.

Another client shared a similar struggle when she would share her pricing. She didn't have the trust and confidence to believe that a potential client would want to pay her full fee, and she kept breaking the silence with a discount.

When I asked her to visualize staying silent after she shared her prices, she couldn't stay focused and see herself doing it. Perhaps when you are struggling with doing something challenging, you can't visualize yourself doing it, either.

Since this client couldn't deal with the silence in the room even in her mind, I had her visualize sharing her prices and then breaking the silence with a lower price. Then we figured out what was going on with her when the potential client didn't quickly respond. She discovered that the silence felt like conflict. She failed to realize that her potential client was quietly considering the proposal.

Once we worked that out, I had her visualize making her offer and then patiently waiting for the other person to respond. She was then able to see herself doing it. Some time later I talked to her about her next consultation after our session. She told me she had nailed the offer without discounting her prices and now has an ideal new client who is excited to get started.

Entrepreneurs use visualization when they are preparing for a difficult conversation. They develop a plan for sticking to their decision. They see themselves reaching out to the other person, sharing their decision, and quickly closing the conversation without lengthy explanations or getting defensive. Then later, when they actually have the conversation, it is not as difficult.

Visualization Can Also Help You To . . .

In addition to helping you prepare to use new techniques, work through difficult situations, develop an action plan, and stay focused, visualization can help you in the following ways.

Cope with the unexpected. The more entrepreneurs advance, the more likely there will be some type of technical glitch or other distraction they can't control. I encourage my clients to visualize not only remaining focused but also unexpected occurrences and how they could respond to them. Then, when something happens that could otherwise rattle them, they are more likely to stay in control and regain their focus more quickly than if they hadn't prepared for those unexpected events. This works even when the actual scenario is not exactly what they had imagined.

Feel confident at new levels and with challenges. As you achieve more success, the difference between the worst and the best company in your industry narrows. You might be confident about always being seen as a success in your current market, but if you move up to the next level and compete with more established businesses, your confidence might suffer or there might be new or unanticipated challenges. Instead of being caught off guard, be proactive. Prepare for your new level by researching the businesses that you are competing against—or could be competing against—and visualize yourself on equal footing with them.

This is especially helpful when you are transitioning, say, from earning under $100,000 to earning low six figures or mid-six figures to crossing the million dollar mark in your business.

Visualization is also helpful if you are adding in a new system or working with a project you find challenging. Practice seeing yourself navigating your way through it. Then, when you actually are doing that activity, you will have done it a hundred times already in your mind, and you will act with more confidence. The action won't be new.

Recover from a setback. If you are recovering from a setback, your goal is to get back into the swing of things.

When you visualize yourself detaching from the setback, gaining insight, and correcting the mistake, you can regain momentum and not spend as much time on dwelling on the mistake. As you see yourself acting with purpose, your muscles will twitch in response to the visualization. You will continue to gain clarity and prepare for new opportunities. It will also give you something positive to focus on, since it is easy to dwell on why things didn't work out as planned and beat yourself up for not preventing the setback.

I feel compelled to add that EFT has been used to speed up the recovery process. Tapping can help remove any self-blame for setbacks and failures, and it works especially well when combined with visualization. In your mind's eye, visualize a new opportunity appearing while using EFT on the tapping points.

Use Visualization to Achieve Your Goal

Perhaps the most powerful way to use visualization is to achieve your goal. I use visualization to help me become clear on my goals and create a positive intention.

You harness the power of visualization by identifying your goal, which must be stated in clear, positive terms. Then, as if you were actually landing that new contract or on the podium receiving a prized award, you see yourself there. If you find visualization challenging, just do your best. With practice, it will get easier.

The intention of visualization is to make your goal and vision feel real, and then, over time, to make it real. If you are truly serious about gaining success, bring visualization into your growth plan. When you do it consistently over time, you will notice the difference. To get you started, try this exercise below.

An Exercise for Visualization
In this exercise, you will be working with a goal or vision. This activity is also available at http://BusinessSuccessSolution.com/book-bonus. Choose a goal or vision that feels a bit out of reach but that you still believe could be achieved. If you choose a performance goal of giving a TED talk by the end of next year and you currently avoid speaking opportunities, that goal might be too far of a stretch. You have to believe your goal is possible, or your visualization won't work. Instead of visualizing, you would be engaging in disbelief.

Instead, perhaps you can see yourself as a breakout speaker during an industry conference within a year. Don't worry about how you are going to get there. Those opportunities will come later.

1. What is your goal?

_____

2. Describe your goal in great detail. Be specific. Saying you want to be a keynote speaker is not specific enough, as there is no emotion attached to it. Instead say, "I want to be speaking to engaged audiences that need to hear my

message" or "I want to speak at a TED conference" or "I want to host my own three-day event."

_____

_____

_____

_____

3. If you were to reach your goal, what qualities, characteristics, and skill sets would you have? To answer this question effectively, it is helpful to study business owners who have reached a similar goal. Until then, imagine their traits. List all the qualities you would have, in all areas of your life. What compromises would you have to make? (If you are speaking on big-name stages, you can't be saying "um" and "you know" all the time.) Be as detailed and descriptive as you can in order to make it feel real to you.

_____

_____

_____

_____

_____

_____

_____

_____

_____

4. Where will you be when you meet your goal? Try to stimulate all of the senses in your mind's eye. For instance, if you are on a TED stage, what does this milestone look like? What does it feel like? What details do you notice? How does it smell? What do you hear? What textures can you feel? The more specific you can get, the better the visualization.

_____

_____

_____

_____

_____

5. By what date do you want to reach your goal? Pick a date that is a little sooner than you would like it to be. People tend to achieve more when there is a little extra stress or tension, so if you move up the date to where it will be a stretch, your effort will be more focused and you will get there sooner.

_____

6. Once you have reached your goal, how will you feel about yourself and your ability? What will be different? How will your business change? How will you feel as you prepare for a keynote speech?

_____

_____

_____

How to Use Your Visualization

Think of the details above as individual scenes, and then string them together to form a movie in your mind's eye of achieving your goal with ease and confidence. This is your visualization.

Now, play it over and over again. I usually have two to three goals at a time, and I visualize each of them twice a day—in the morning before I get out of bed and in the evening as I am going to sleep. A visualization on a very specific thing can take a couple of seconds. The visualization described above will probably take you five to ten minutes.

If that sounds like a big commitment, think about your growth strategy. How often do you work on advancing your business? How many hours, weeks, months, and years are put into preparing for your future success? The more you prepare and the more you repeat it, the more that specific pathway in your brain is strengthened so that you respond from a familiar, knowing place with ease and confidence when your defining moment arrives.

The same is true for visualization. As you do it, you come to believe in it more and more, you move closer to your goal, and viewing yourself as a successful entrepreneur becomes more natural to you.

A One-Two Punch: Combining Visualization with EFT

People often do not really believe they can achieve their goals. As they visualize, they still have some doubt in the back of their mind. If you follow your visualization with EFT, you can neutralize the doubt on the spot.

When I work with a client, I frequently combine the two techniques. I did so with my social media marketer client who wasn't comfortable with sales conversations. Instead of remaining quiet after she shared her prices, she discounted her rates. Now, this is a person who has very high expectations of her abilities, and as a respected professional in her community, wanted to help business owners attract new clients. When she got to asking them to invest in her services, though, she wasn't able to shake off her discomfort, and her confidence was shaken.

With EFT, we worked on her frustration, anger, and disappointment associated with repeating this behavior over and over again. Using EFT, we first tapped on the self-critical thoughts for caving into the pressure in the first place. Saying those statements aloud while tapping lessened their intensity, and after a while, they just didn't feel true to her anymore.

After dealing with the negative thoughts, we focused on her strengths, continuing to use the tapping to cement in her positive qualities. Then, using visualization with EFT, we restructured her memory. I had her go through the sales conversation as she would like to see it play out. This lessened the intensity of emotion because now, in her mind's eye, she got to maintain composure the way she meant to during those critical moments.

EFT and visualization work immediately. One night, I called the photographer who ended up becoming a client just to introduce myself. She told me about her anxiety when meeting with prospective clients. She mentioned that an important meeting was scheduled with a potential client the next morning. I asked her if she would like to remove her doubts, and she said yes. She didn't know me. She had never used EFT before, but she was willing to try it.

This is lesson one of this story: be open to opportunities when they arise. You never know. Someone could just call you out of the blue.

We talked for ten minutes about her core issue regarding rejection and then did some tapping around it. While she tapped, I asked her to visualize how she wanted the meeting to turn out. Then I helped her with her mindset and made suggestions of what to focus on before the meeting started. The ability to access this zone at will changed her mindset from dread to anticipation. She was now excited to show this company how she could help increase their website sales.

A couple of days later, I got an email from her telling me that not only did she get the contract, but she had landed her biggest client and earned $3,500 on that one deal!

I have to agree that that is impressive, but the much more powerful part of the story is that we both saw opportunity and took it. What if I hadn't followed my intuition to call her? That would have been on me. And what if she hadn't been willing to try something new? Given what her year had been like, she probably wouldn't have achieved those results the next day, and she would have walked away from that meeting on a low note and with less confidence for not getting that vendor contract. The second lesson from this story is to seize opportunities even when the timing may be inconvenient.

When my client started the new year, she almost barely believed she could reach her goals. In fact, she told me she was on the verge of walking away from her photography business. Now she is on the verge of expanding her team. I am not saying that using EFT and visualization can increase your income, but they can give you emotional distance from what troubles and distracts you and get you several steps closer to your goal.

To find out for yourself how EFT and visualization work, try the exercise in appendix V, which walks you through combining the two.

Seeing yourself as a successful entrepreneur is not about how others see you, it is about how you see yourself. If your heart is in helping your clients, if you are committed to excellence and ready to do whatever it takes, nothing can get in your way unless you allow it to.

Seeing yourself as a success is truly about living your dream. I believe this is why people revere motivational leaders. These leaders pursue their dreams and turn them into realities, whereas most people leave their dreams behind too soon. Motivational leaders offer hope that anything is possible   .

Part Three: Act Like a Successful Entrepreneur

7: How to Act Like a Successful Entrepreneur

Sometimes you have to grow into a position. Acting like a success helps you grow into *being* a success. What does it mean to act like a success? How do successful entrepreneurs act?

The obvious difference is successful entrepreneurs go into business with the intention to succeed as opposed to having the focus of "not failing." They have a different perception, frame of reference, and mentality. Successful entrepreneurs don't necessarily see failure as others do; they know they can grow from every experience. They are passionate, always open to learning, and perhaps most surprising, they know that they don't know it all.

If you have made it this far into the book, then you have at least one vital success quality—the willingness to learn. As for the rest, it is not as though you either have it or you don't. You can learn the other traits. In fact, at some colleges, business majors take a personality type test to see if they have the characteristics of a successful business owner, and if they don't have them yet, they work on developing those things.

In other words, you can learn how to be a successful entrepreneur, and acting like you have already achieved success is a great way to start.

The Secrets to Acting Like a Successful Entrepreneur

Start now. A lot of people say, "When *this* happens, *then* I will make some changes." They put off into the future what they could be doing now. Does that future ever come? Often, no.

Ask yourself what you could be doing *now* to step into being a successful entrepreneur. This chapter will give you some ideas to help get you started.

Recently, I asked a business consultant why so few business owners survive beyond the first five years. He said some part of it has to do with luck. I disagree. Luck has nothing to do with it. It has to do with how someone shows up, how they recognize opportunities (if they even do), and how they create the opportunities to make the "luck" happen.

Let's say a spa has three massage therapists, and one person is getting booked more than the other two. What differentiates her from the massage therapists with holes in their schedules? What specific qualities do successful massage therapists share? Those with successful careers rely on more than their charm. They love what they do, genuinely care about their clients, and continuously seeks ways to improve their skills.

If you want to be booked solid, ask yourself what your ideal clients and potential referral partners are looking for that you could offer in your practice.

Study successful entrepreneurs. How do you figure out what potential clients and referral partners are looking for? You could ask, but more importantly, observe and study successful entrepreneurs in your industry as well as those business owners who have already achieved the goal you have set for yourself. What practices do these entrepreneurs follow? What do they offer their ideal clients? How do they advance their skills? How are their lifestyles congruent with consistently delivering an exceptional product or service?

These top entrepreneurs live differently during and after business hours than you do. They prepare differently. They might have different ways of taking care of themselves—how they prepare for upcoming deadlines, how they manage their self-care, and how they develop strategic alliances. There will be nuances, too, and you won't know what those things are unless you study these highly successful business owners. Once you find those nuances, see what small adjustments you can begin making now toward the goal of living and continuing to develop as they do. Bring these details into your visualization. As you see yourself in your mind's eye doing what they do, you will make incremental changes, and your actions will start to shift.

Becoming aware of the day-to-day realities of those business owners will also help you in several other ways:

- You will be prepared to deal with any challenges you will face later. You won't be surprised, for example, by what you have to give up.

- You will learn the qualities strategic alliances are looking for, and, as a result, you will advance at a faster rate or gain recognition.

- You will develop confidence, and confidence is a boost that gives your business an unfair advantage over your competitors. Let's just be honest about that.

The bottom line is, if you have a vision of what you want to accomplish, then why not do everything within your power to tilt the odds in your favor?

Create your own opportunities. One of the keys to tilting the odds in your favor is to create your own opportunities. You can't wait around to be discovered you have to be proactive.

If you have your eyes set on improving your industry standards, and you are currently in the start-up phase and want to be recognized by industry leaders, what can you do to get noticed? It depends on how much presence you are creating. If you are busy working in your business most of the time, then being involved in professional organizations becomes important. You never know where an opportunity may appear. To get even more attention, join a national organization where recognized leaders attend industry conferences. Get involved on a committee. Act decisively, but make your associates look good, as well.

Even if you are not an outgoing leader, it is still possible to gain recognition. Passion trumps abilities.

Having your heart in advancing your profession, knowing how to deal with adversity and having the willingness to consistently improve your skills are qualities of successful entrepreneurs. Natural talent will take you only so far, but talent alone is not enough. Talent must be combined with a strong, deep motivation to take yourself the full distance.

If you feel ready to get involved or would like to be in a more substantial leadership role, the best thing to do is to talk to the decision-makers about how to best utilize your skills. Discover what qualities those decision-makers seek when they are looking to fill key positions. Learn what you need to do to be considered. If someone better is already in that position, observe that person. Where does he or she excel? What can you do to get recognized as an asset?

Sometimes enthusiasm sells. Sometimes a leader doesn't see a person as having the capabilities to even be considered seriously, but if he or she is passionate about wanting to get involved, then the passion overrides the lack of obvious capabilities. The bottom line is, when you start looking to create opportunities, they will appear.

Practice good self-care. If you are looking to be a "go-to" expert, mental clarity is not optional. Along with clarity come insights, and insights spring from intuition. Alcohol and recreational drugs impair your intuition as well as your emotional awareness, and just as with athletes, maintaining your physical health is important. Highly successful entrepreneurs are high performers.

Exercise and physical strength keep your body at its best for intense, demanding circumstances.

I am not a nutritionist, so I will just say that entrepreneurs should eat certain foods and avoid others. Obvious examples to avoid include soda, energy drinks, chips, high doses of caffeine, fried foods, fast food, and highly processed foods. Of course, avoid tobacco products, too. Respect your body as your vehicle, and treat it well. If you want to be a high-performing entrepreneur, eat like one and keep your mind clear.

Use keywords. Keywords are quick affirmations, easy reminders of your vision. They create focus and are particularly useful for deciding if an opportunity will advance your business or is actually a distraction.

Keywords work as reminders. For example, Amy is a bookkeeper who is building her practice. She chose "steady growth and strength" as her reminder phrase, or keywords. Now when opportunities appear, she determines whether those activities will help to advance her business and utilize her strengths. Amy's keywords help her to decide whether an opportunity is aligned with her goal or not.

To use a keyword, simply pair a simple word with a particular outcome to keep yourself focused on the goal. The more you practice using your keyword to keep you on course, the more effective it will be. The keyword creates a new neural pathway in your brain, which is activated when you repeat it while doing an activity that will help you advance your business. It is a form of muscle memory. By creating an association, the word creates a behavioral response.

For example, developing strong relationships is something I continually strive to do. When I am focused on the things I need to do to meet the right people, such as which conferences to attend, who I want to meet, and how to meet the right people, the introvert side of me reminds me that I prefer small, intimate gatherings. I really want to avoid big, noisy settings. I simply remember that my primary keywords are *connection* and *invitation*. As I meet with people, I am reminded that I want to have a meaningful conversation with them, and if it seems like a good connection, then I suggest we set a time to talk again. As a result, I am more relaxed in large settings. I trust that I will meet the exact right people at an event instead of trying to meet everyone, and I find that more enjoyable.

One of my financial advisor clients uses keywords to help with pacing his speech during presentations. If he feels anxious about a specific presentation, he rushes through the presentation, which affects his connection to his audience. Also, if he falters early in his presentation, it throws him off for the rest of the talk; he never recovers his focus.

To help him with those problems, we came up with a ritual to remind him to breathe, relax, and use keywords to help him refocus when in front of an audience. He uses his keywords, *relax* and *present,* before even taking a step into the room where he will be presenting. He also uses them quietly in his head during his presentation if he loses focus. The keywords remind him to compose himself, put the mistake behind him, and refocus on delivering a great presentation to his audience.

I use both keywords and EFT in my work with an organizational consultant who is very talented and is transitioning from being an employee to owning his own agency but gets easily frustrated because of his high expectations. He gets angry and impatient, and his focus and decision-making are affected. His behavior was impacting his work, and control issues kept him from getting assistance.

We came up with the keywords *power* and *focus,* which remind him how he wants to be in his business. Using the words retrains his brain. He remembers not to take it personally when things don't go as planned. If he makes a mistake, it is not about him as a person, it is about a set of actions he takes.

As a result of using keywords, he became more relaxed and was able to let go of perfecting something that otherwise would have consumed extra hours without affecting the final result. As a result of using both keywords and EFT, his anger response changed. He now has more fun and has hired several contract workers to help him out.

If you would like to start using keywords right away, see the exercise below.

An Exercise for How to Use Keywords

Keep it simple. We often want to complicate things, but with keywords, simple will get you the best results.

Knowing what you want to achieve is the first step in choosing a keyword or words that will work for you.

Choose one or two words that have meaning to you about your actions. Choose as few words as possible. We don't have the capacity to track and maintain focus on a lot of different things, and changing one or two things at a time is enough. Put your focus on those one or two things you really want to do.

Try out your word or words, connecting them to a specific activity, as I did with networking. Be willing to modify them, if necessary. You are now ready to start using your keywords to help you be the business owner you want to be. The handout, "How to Use Keywords," is available at http://BusinessSuccessSolution.com/book-bonus.

You Can Do It

If you are still wondering whether you can successfully apply these tools on your own, let me tell you about the loan officer who came to one of my seminars.

She had been ranked the number one producer in the state but had gone into a sales slump. It had gotten to the point where her work was not enjoyable for her anymore, so she took two years off, which in her industry is significant. She switched to another firm but had still not achieved the new loan applications she knew she was capable of, that were needed to get recognized as a top regional seller, and that would justify adding on another assistant.

At the seminar, I talked about acting "as if," using visualization and keywords, and coming up with an action plan. The following month, I got a call from her. She told me she had her best month ever with this company and had achieved the new loan applications goal she had set for herself. If she can get those results after attending a two-hour seminar, you can get results, too.

8: Act "As If"

One of the most effective ways to achieve your goal is to act "as if" you already have. You really take it in that you already are the success you want to be, and then you behave and make choices as though the future you want is occurring right now. Acting as if helps you evolve to your next level of success.

When you act as if, you have already achieved your goal and how you look at and respond to situations transforms. You realize you can choose how you want to act or react.

Old beliefs will start to come up and get in your way. If you are truly committed, be open to looking at those beliefs to determine whether they are something you want to hold on to or modify.

For example, Alex, one of my web developer clients, questioned whether he could raise his rates. I told him that thinking he could only charge by the hour was limiting his income because hourly pricing overlooked his years of experience in the field and he was faster at website design now than when he first started out.

Alex's belief that "an honest day's work for an honest day's pay" was getting in the way of earning what he was really worth, and he was open to another view. We discussed how he always charged by the hour, yet earning his ideal income meant working more hours than he wanted to.

This brought up memories of his corporate job. He earned a good salary while working at that job. High stress due to long hours and high expectations, however, affected him and his family. He believed that "if I don't handle stress, then I'm a failure." Those thoughts triggered a specific incident that caused him to leave his job.

Alex was willing to modify his belief about pricing for his services, and he did it through EFT and reframing. We couldn't change his history, but we could stop him from getting triggered. EFT is a tool that helped Alex release the anger and failure connected to that specific event. The tapping helped him to emotionally distance himself from the incident. Finally, he was at peace with the event.

Now he was ready to discuss ways to earn more without working harder. Value-based pricing was the solution. This pricing model emphasized the value of achieving a specific result instead of the amount of hours he spent on a project. Alex had to believe in his worth before he could switch to value-based pricing. First he acknowledged that his website design generated revenue for his clients. Then we worked on developing packages and programs with the new pricing model.

Several months later, Alex walked into my office, beaming. I asked, "Alex, you look like you won the lottery. What happened?" He said, "I deposited twelve thousand dollars from a new client yesterday. He signed up for my new package and paid for the program in full."

Alex finally realized that he could earn his ideal income without overwhelm.

Make a Breakthrough Acting As If

In an earlier chapter, I encouraged you to learn to love what you avoid. Acting as if is a great way to accomplish this. Some entrepreneurs bill after they have helped their clients, then complain about chasing money or not getting paid on time, which affects their cash flow. I encourage my clients who are uncomfortable discussing payment to envision getting paid before they start working with a new client. They experience how things would be different if they became more comfortable with asking for payment.

When my clients learn to love getting paid before their clients start with them, they won't spend tons of time collecting on outstanding bills. While others are complaining, my clients enjoy greater prosperity. They are happy, and they aren't bothered with writing off someone who will never pay. This definitely shifts their mindset about their value.

Some clients recognize that they need to alter their beliefs about money and self-worth. Without even trying, my clients attract better clients because of this. During the process, they also learn to own their value and gain clarity about how they help, which separates them from other business owners in their industry.

This strategy is effective for any entrepreneur whose primary concern is to make a difference for their clients, and the money is secondary.

Remember, making friends with what you don't like is extremely helpful for any challenge you are facing. Instead of looking at the situation as an obstacle affecting your business, act as if you love it. This will begin to shift your perspective dramatically and enable you to rise to the challenge and overcome it with ease.

A Tool for Acting As If

A powerful tool for acting as if is intention setting. An intention is a goal brought to life by connecting strong, powerful emotions to it. This creates focus and fire and an almost magnetic energy that starts to draw opportunities toward you. Results come at a quicker pace than with goal setting alone.

Unlike goal setting—which tends to be sterile, with a problem and objective, activities, a beginning date and an ending date—an intention is a mindset strategy for utilizing positive focus and expectation to achieve your goals.

If you had trouble with the visualization exercise, it might help you to start here, with your intention. Once you create your story of how to reach your goal, you might find it easier to visualize the end result. Also, if talking is easier than writing, you can record and transcribe your intention (and your visualization), which will give you both a verbal and a written version.

I have mindset, business, and personal intentions. Some intentions are just for one day, while others are longer term. For the following exercise, choose the category and timeframe that appeal to you.

An Exercise to Create Your Intention

1. Decide what your goal is. You can use the same one you used for the visualization exercise, or you can choose a different goal.

_____

_____

_____

2. What is your challenge in relation to your goal? What are you facing? Where are you stuck?

_____

_____

_____

3. Choose three to five action steps you could take to reach your goal.

_____

_____

_____

_____

_____

_____

4. As you did in the visualization exercise, create a story for each action step. How do you feel about it? What are the circumstances surrounding the step? What is the environment around you? Who is there with you? Who isn't? Make each story as rich in detail as you can. The richer the better, and the more you can bring your senses into it, the more your story will come alive.

_____

_____

_____

_____

_____

_____

_____

_____

_____

_____

_____

_____

_____

_____

5. Together, these stories comprise your intention. They form a highly personal story of achieving your goal, similar to the storyline of a movie.

There are two schools of thought on what to do with your intention. One says to write it and forget it, letting your subconscious mind do the work. The other says read the intention every day, keeping it front and center in your conscious mind. Use the approach that makes the most sense to you.

Feel free to modify your intention as your situation changes. Your intention should be a living document.

Desire Is More Important than Knowledge

If you are looking to attract more clients, set your next goal and create your next intention before reaching your current goal. This reinforces the idea that if you can dream it, it is possible. You don't have to know all the different action steps needed to reach your next goal. Just get started with what you do know, and the steps will come up at the appropriate time. Having a strong, burning desire is much more important than knowing how to get there.

This is a real-life David and Goliath story. Warby Parker, an online eyewear company, is commonly viewed as a business that successfully challenged the industry giant, Luxottica, yet many expected the business to fail. The concept to sell affordable eyeglasses online was inspired by four business school students on a backpacking trip, during which one of them lost his glasses. The cost to replace them was so high that he couldn't afford a new pair during his first semester of grad school, so he chose to squint instead. These four friends worked on their business idea during their spare time between classes, internships, and jobs. They tested and surveyed and fine-tuned their plan.

Eventually, the team was ready to go live with their business, although many experts doubted they would survive. When they finally opened for business, the company reached their annual sales goal within the first three weeks of launching.

Instead of taking risks, they took their time. They hedged their bets by keeping their day jobs and all their options open. They reduced costs by cutting out the middleman, designing their own frames, and working directly with manufacturers.

Now *that* is dedication—continuing with school and working day jobs to maintain their belief that everyone has a right to see.

You may not have such a dramatic story, but I bet you have your own burning desire for your business. Bring it into your intention. The more you attach strong emotion to your intention, the more powerful it will be.

Uplevel

Another tool for acting as if is called upleveling. In this context, upleveling means to upgrade aspects of your actions to reflect the next level of what you are striving toward. You start to make changes now to affect how you feel about yourself and the way you and your business are perceived. Those changes may be small, mundane, and inexpensive, or they might require investing in something to position your business for success.

One of the most powerful uplevels you can do is to spend time with and learn from entrepreneurs who are more advanced than you. If you are earning under $100,000 and you want to earn a six-figure income, talk with an entrepreneur who has already achieved that level of success. You don't know how entrepreneurs at the next level do things unless you spend time with them.

The differences between what an entrepreneur with a multi-six figure income is doing and what you are doing will probably be eye-opening, because as a business grows, the difference between the best and the worst narrows. There will be nuances or fine-tuning you can apply to your business immediately. There will be things you didn't even know you weren't doing. Associating with a business owner who has already achieved the level of success that you are working toward is a great way to find out what you don't yet know.

If mentoring with that person is not possible, reach out by email or phone and see if you can have a conversation, or get together at a conference. Some business owners will be open to helping you, and others won't.

If the business owner is not open to helping, observe him when you are at a common event. Notice who he talks to and whether he networks differently from you. Does he use the free time between sessions differently from you? What do you notice about him that you could model?

Look for what he is doing and also what he is *not* doing. That is often much more telling. Is he *not* spending a lot of time networking? Not interested in collecting business cards, like everybody else does? If so, he might have a strategy to connect with specific individuals.

Remember, traditional tactics work for the average business owner. If you want to be extraordinary, you have to act differently. Highly successful business owners often modify their agenda to what is best suited for them.

Once you have found your successful business owner and know some things you didn't know before, see how you can modify the information to make it work for you. You might find that you don't want to do some of the things he does, but others things will be gems. Even a small change can make a significant difference in your approach and confidence. You might find yourself willing to do things you weren't willing to do before.

For instance, when I was interviewed as an expert by the *Los Angeles Times* to comment on the television show *Necessary Roughness*, I felt empowered to reach out to people who were better known in the field and to possible business partners I didn't feel comfortable reaching out to before.

The media recognition affected my perception. My business would pop up on an Internet search! The public credibility boosted my confidence, which boosted my courage to contact several entrepreneurs whom I had formerly believed were out of my league.

You might find that your upleveling experience empowers you, too, to take risks you shied away from in the past.

Change Is Significant

Whether big or small, any changes you make will be significant, but acting as if isn't always comfortable. You may find yourself outside of your comfort zone, stretching yourself. A success mindset will prepare you for taking those necessary steps for success, no matter how uncomfortable you might feel.

Your change will lead to growth, which can be rapid. Too often, entrepreneurs are not ready for fast growth, and they act out to sabotage it. There is an implosion effect. What do I mean by that? Well, when something happens too quickly and the foundation is not in place, it is likely to fall apart. It becomes messy because some things might not have been foreseen and prepared for, which leads to failure or major setbacks.

The best way to handle growth is to know you don't have to do it all on your own. Go find the right support. Where to find the support you need is the subject of the next chapter.

9: Choose Your Best Network

Entrepreneurs are not islands unto themselves. They typically don't operate alone, figure it all out by themselves, or mentor themselves to success.

Who Is In Your Network?

Your network is actually a big group. It includes all of the people you associate with: your mentors and industry leaders, employees, associates you turn to for help in working through a challenge, other support people, family, and friends.

The members of your network have the power to raise you up or bring you down. If you have support people who are always negative or critical of you, you can easily get discouraged. Some people have the fight in them to prove the doubters wrong, but I have seen entrepreneurs throw in the towel because after they have been beaten down enough, they begin to believe they are failures.

Sometimes the lack of support is subtle. For instance, family members might be supportive of you in general, but they might not believe in your dream or your big goals as strongly as you do, or perhaps one of your goals competes with theirs. For instance, if your marketing schedule requires you to travel and your spouse wants you to stay home, there is a conflict, and the support you need may not be there. Or family members might say things like, "Are you sure you want to do that?" or "You might not want to do this because maybe you won't succeed."

You need to understand where these responses originate. Those family members want you to have your vision, but they are afraid that seeing you frustrated or disappointed when you don't meet your expectations will be uncomfortable for *them*, and they won't know how to deal with it.

When you get frustrated or disappointed, they believe they are supposed to do something about it—but it is not their purpose or responsibility. Their purpose in your life is to validate the experience you are having and to support you in doing whatever is necessary and right for you, not what *they* believe is right for you. Nobody is the expert on your life or what you need more than you are.

It is important for you to absorb good advice and insight from other people, but the bottom line is, you need to make decisions for yourself. If you don't take an opportunity, you are the one who may spend the rest of your life wondering, *What if?*

Not long ago, I met with a business owner who had some confidence issues. She had an opportunity to attend a professional association conference, but the thought of going alone was intimidating. I asked, "Have there been other networking opportunities you missed because they were uncomfortable?" She admitted, "I said no to several speaking opportunities."

Those speaking gigs may have led to new business. We spoke about patterns of behavior and how they work. I explained, "These behaviors are like an Achilles heel.

They hold you back from doing something uncomfortable." She recognized some parallel processes occurring, and she wants to do it different this time.

If you have confidence issues, if you hold back, if you are afraid of change, those things will likely come up again and again until you look at why they happen and decide to modify the underlying beliefs to those more appropriate for your life right now.

Does Your Network Mirror the Success in You?

> *You are the average of the*
> *five people you spend the*
> *most time with.*
> —Jim Rohn

Does the quote above scare you? If so, you might want to consider this section carefully. The people you surround yourself with affect your mindset. If you spend time with people who are forward thinkers and who understand your excitement and drive, you are in good company.

You want to connect with people who are already achieving some of the goals you are currently striving for. If you want to be a millionaire, you need to spend time with millionaires. They think and act different from people who live paycheck to paycheck.

The same is true of highly successful entrepreneurs. If you want to achieve a higher level of potential than you are currently achieving, start spending time with entrepreneurs who are already at that level. Befriend them. Hang out with them. Notice how they spend their time. Notice what they do and don't do.

On the other hand, if you are surrounded by people who are always in one crisis after another and you seem to be the solution to their problems, your energy will be drained. Or if you are very driven and want to stretch yourself but others in your business don't share your vision—maybe it is solely financial for them—you are not likely to advance your business as quickly as you would were you surrounded by people who have the same ambition as you. This is particularly true of family-owned businesses or when a business partner is involved. This can lead to frustration and resentment on your part and affect the culture of your business.

One of the most difficult things to do but necessary to move forward is to take a hard look at the people in your life and see if you have some difficult decisions to make about keeping them. Highly dedicated entrepreneurs sometimes feel conflicted when they have to make difficult decisions about who to spend time with, whether it is friends, family, clients, or associates. They are moving on, and sometimes they have to create distance between themselves and people they are attached to emotionally; otherwise, the relationships would sabotage their goals. This is not easy to do. But as my husband, Steve Fogelman, says, "You measure personal growth by the people you leave behind."

You may have to limit contact with people who bring you down or who can't support your vision 100 percent or who drain your energy.

There may be people in your life you care about, in your family, perhaps, whom you are not going to cut out of your life entirely. In these cases, it is even more important to set boundaries with them and have a strong support system of positive people around you.

When you are on your journey toward excellence, you must have positive people in your network, people who share in your dream, because you will definitely face obstacles and challenges along the way. And although you are persevering, if you are not having the results or seeing the progress you expect, doubt might begin to creep in. That is when your group of supporters, those who really believe in you and your vision, are so important. They will lift you up when you can't hold yourself up.

If you don't have those positive people in your life who can help you refocus on your strengths, then when you get frustrated, the negative people in your life, who so easily point out flaws and criticize, might reinforce your doubt, digging it in deeper, which will keep you in the place of doubt longer than is necessary.

Yes, I wrote "necessary." When you are feeling doubt, you might actually be at the threshold of a breakthrough but can't see it. Your supportive people, however, are able to partner with you to help you process through what is happening and what is preventing you from taking the leap of faith in front of you. They might also take the leap with you. Remember, you don't have to do this on your own.

We all need people in our network to help us see what we can't. Few of us can see what is right under our nose. We get caught up in our own story, and it is hard to see it from another perspective.

How Supportive Relationships Help

There is a classic psychological concept called the Johari window, which explains the power of any supportive relationship, including marriage.

Picture a window with four quadrants. In the first quadrant are the things you know about yourself and that others know about you, too. These are easily observable things, such as what you look like.

In the second quadrant are your secrets. You know these things about yourself, but I don't. For instance, you may eat a pint of ice cream every night or watch a soap opera every day. These are things you may not want anyone else to know.

In the third quadrant are hidden things. You might not know these things about yourself, but I do. Although it is subconscious, body language is stronger than the spoken word. For example, if you are anxious about your upcoming presentation, you might nervously tap your right foot without realizing it. Another hidden thing is my opinion about you.

The fourth quadrant contains the unknown. These are the things you don't know about yourself, and neither do I. These are your subconscious thoughts, dreams you don't recall, repressed memories, and things that happened when you were dissociated or "spaced out."

As you work with a business coach (or a counselor or other supportive person), unknown, hidden, and secret things come out into the open, and the third and fourth quadrants get smaller while the first one becomes more expansive. Through insight, feedback, and processing, you become aware of things about yourself you never would have known, and you take what you do know to a deeper level. The result is a more expansive open window for you. Supportive relationships have the power to help us grow tremendously.

What If You Are Surrounded by Negativity?

Who wouldn't want a cadre of people helping them at every turn? But what do you do if you don't have positive support in your life right now? What if the only one who believes in your dream is you? If so, don't despair. Remember Oprah Winfrey? Early in her career, she was informed that she was unfit for television, but she believed in herself and kept going.

Your own support is a potent beginning. Now you can start looking for your support network. If you look, you will find. In the meantime, here are a few other practices to help you and to strengthen your skills.

Learn how to cope with a negative business partner. Having a business partner who truly knows how to motivate you and believes in you even when you can't believe in yourself is very powerful. Too often, however, business partners focus on what you are not doing well. They don't always realize you need to be told what you are doing well, too.

A human resources client felt that her performance was being hampered by her business partner during client consultations because the business partner was telling her only what not to do, where not to offer input. My client believed the negative criticism was defeating the purpose of their relationship and causing her effectiveness to suffer.

Another business partner I heard about threatens to stop contributing when improvement doesn't happen fast enough, but his business partners weren't offered feedback on how they could improve their results; they were being told only what not to do.

Negative criticism is counterproductive, and focusing on the negative enhances the negative. If you want to improve, you have to focus on areas to improve. To me, this is common sense, and it is borne out by the most recent neuroscience.

If your business partner is negative, there are ways to cope with it. I discussed some of this before, but it bears repeating. First and foremost, understand that your business partner truly wants you to succeed. Your success directly impacts him or her.

Second, rather than avoiding the issue and letting frustration build up or blaming your business partner, look for solutions. Try to communicate your experience to your partner, who may not realize the negative impact his or her words have on you. If you need something from your partner you are not getting, like with my pediatric nutritionist client, find someone who can help you with that aspect of your skill set.

Third, if you can't switch business partners, look past the negativity to find the gem in the feedback. I encouraged my human resources client to take the gist of the advice to see how her partner was trying to support her or encourage her even though it was coming out the wrong way. I also told her it was a great opportunity to learn how to not let anybody else's energy or negativity get under her skin and affect her actions.

When you can learn to do the same with the negative people in your life, you are one step closer to the freedom that comes from not being negatively affected by what other people do or say. When you look at the negative people in your life as opportunities, or inducements, to build your own support network, you can thrive in any environment.

Set the tone for your day. When you spend time with people who tend to be critical or negative, you might not even realize they are being that way, because you become so used to it. On the other hand, when you spend time with people who are positive and really doing something for themselves or believe in what you are doing, you will have a much better frame of mind and experience.

One of the ways to control your environment and not let others' negativity affect you is to set your own tone for the day. Do you start the day reading or listening to all the doom and gloom in the news? If so, that is the tone you are setting for the rest of the morning and even the day.

When you start your day with how people are struggling and not doing well, your brain reinforces that message by looking for struggle and things not going well. However, when you avoid reading the newspaper or listening to the news early in the day, you will set yourself up for a much more positive experience.

You can take this idea further by choosing to start your day with an intention, visualization, meditation, workout, or some other aspect of self-care. When you do this, you consciously set the tone for your day with action steps toward your goal, which will have a positive effect on the rest of your day.

Don't take my word on this. Do an experiment and see for yourself. If you tend to listen to the news every morning, for the next week, notice how you feel and act after listening to the news and how long it affects you. The following week, instead of digesting the news, read or listen to something motivational. See if you notice the difference in how you act, how you respond to people, and how you feel about the state of the union.

Create an internal support system. Whether or not you are surrounded by negative people, being able to refer to an internal support system is powerful. It is almost like having your own personal board of directors.

What do I mean? First, I want you to open your mind, because this might sound weird at first. I can tell you, though, it works. I suggest that you visualize yourself sitting with the mentors you would choose to have as your guides, imagine having conversations with them, and then listen to their insights. You would be surprised by the information you can garner this way.

Think of it as your virtual King Arthur's Round Table, and all these people are there to help support you and give you insights and guidance toward your goal. Who would be sitting at your inner round table?

The truth is, intuition is part of the process as you work toward excellence in whatever you do. When you were fixing a complicated problem, how many times did you just "know" to make a minor tweak or that a seemingly unrelated aspect was the key to correcting the problem? That insight wasn't based on anything conscious, you just "knew." You can tap into this knowing anytime you want.

Your inner round table is especially helpful when you are facing doubts, which is when you may start saying critical things to yourself, a practice you likely inherited from the people who raised you. Some part of you is pointing out all the reasons why you should back down and why you are not supposed to be doing this, or how you don't deserve it. Doesn't it make sense to replace the practice you inherited with a committee of your own choosing, who will champion for you and help guide you?

In his book *Think and Grow Rich*, Napoleon Hill describes nightly meetings with his inner board of directors, which was composed of figures from history. Through their conversations, he gained insights and wisdom to help guide him on his personal journey.

If you would like to give your inner round table a try, here is an exercise to get you started.

An Exercise for How to Create Your Own Inner Round Table

1. Make a list of the people you admire most and whom you would like as guides. They can be living or deceased, famous or not. You can have as many as you want, but in the beginning, aim for around five to keep it simple.

2. Don't get hung up on where the information is coming from or whether it is "real." If you gain insights you wouldn't have had otherwise, what does it matter where it originates? The bottom line is, you are able to access a deeper knowledge within yourself by going through this process than if you never go through it. It is one more way to step out of the box.

3. Sit down, close your eyes, imagine your group sitting around the table, and start asking questions. Ask a specific question, relax, and note what pops up. Forcing something usually gives the opposite result and prevents the tool from working.

   It is better not to take notes, because you might distract yourself from the visualization. Just write down your insights or "ahas" soon afterward.

4. If you draw a blank or have other difficulty, keep trying anyway. After a week of practice, you will probably find yourself suddenly engaging in conversations with your round table while you are in the shower or going for a run.

Don't despair if you don't get immediate results. As with all new things, there is a learning curve, and it requires patience and practice. Remember, this strategy strengthens your intuition, or gut feeling. If you haven't exercised that muscle before, remember that it just takes time. Once you get the hang of it, this will be one of your best self-coaching tools.

If this tool doesn't work for you after a week or so, you can always scrap it. But if it does work, you will have one more tool to give you an edge you didn't have before.

Adopt the Mantle of Success

This section has been about the merits of acting like a success and how to do so. I have explained how acting as if you are already a successful entrepreneur changes your focus. You start looking for opportunities and how you can push yourself, perhaps by taking action where you normally wouldn't. How you perceive your surroundings changes.

Acting as if you are a success also focuses your energy in a positive way, and you show up with more confidence, which your associates will sense. Not only does acting as if you are already a success change how you see yourself, but it changes how other professionals see you, as well.

Part Four:
Be the Successful
Entrepreneur
You Want to Be

10: Begin Right Now

To be the successful entrepreneur you want to be, I urge you to start combining the points I have given you in this book, but don't do it in a way that overwhelms you. You don't have to do it all at one time or perfectly.

These are the three most important changes to make right away:

1. Change your belief system. The changes that need to be made in your belief system may have already come up for you. What are they? You could ask yourself: What situation would I like to look at differently? How would I prefer to view it? How can I begin to make that change?

2. Believe in your goals. Look at your goals and really begin to believe they are possible. Then, instead of focusing on how much you will have to work to get there or wondering whether you ever will get there, start looking for opportunities to meet your goals. Your goals may be a stretch for you, but if you are fully committed, you will get there.

3. Incorporate your research. Once you have done your research on how highly successful entrepreneurs in your profession think differently and how they approach self-care—which is not the same as how they *do* things—find a couple of action steps you can begin to incorporate now that will make you feel like a success. They can be as simple as investing in new clothes for your wardrobe or joining a networking group that successful business owners belong to. Perhaps you wouldn't normally invest the money for these things because you don't feel you can afford them yet, but if you go ahead and make the investment and use them now, your confidence will rise a notch. You will start to feel like a success. You will start to grow into your bigger vision of yourself.

All of these incremental changes, when combined with actions that continue to advance your business, will build on themselves. They will come together and create exponential, positive results.

Please note that you do have to use these concepts along with your action plan. No matter how powerful your mindset is, you cannot achieve success if you don't prepare for it, because you won't have the infrastructure in place to sustain it. Your systems have to be in place. Having a success mindset *in tandem* with the ability to deliver results is what positions you as a go-to expert.

Outcome versus Performance Goals

Most entrepreneurs have outcome goals for money, service, and growth. They want to earn more money or develop a new product or gain new clients. Outcome goals are helpful to know whether you are hitting the numbers; however, I urge you to put most of your attention on execution and action goals, on *how* you are doing what you are doing. Unlike outcome goals, which may depend in part on the market, timing, and other external factors, execution goals involve things you can completely control: your mindset and your actions. What execution goal do you want to focus on first?

One execution goal might be to help potential new clients make the best decision about whether to work with you. Your goal could also be about your self-talk and composure. Set a specific goal for whatever is appropriate for you.

Also set goals based on technical ability, focusing on those things you have complete control over. Is there a particular skill set you could develop further, knowing that it will improve your overall effectiveness? Look at your leadership style, negotiation skills, and boundaries. Your goals may be around networking, public speaking, or sales consultations. Decide what you want to focus on first.

As a result of focusing on your execution goals, you will actually be more likely to reach your outcome goals, because execution goals are empowering. With an outcome goal, you either hit it or not. You succeed or you fail. But an execution goal is about the process, about improving, and that keeps you moving forward.

When you are overly focused on your outcome goal, your cash flow, your monthly quota, or a bid against another business for a contract, you can be distracted, which affects your better judgment. When you are thinking, *I have to land this new client to make payroll on time,* you are not in the moment. You feel anxiety because you are not focused on what is important right now. You tense up, and your effectiveness drops. This is an example of a thought's direct impact on your actions, and it can happen in a split second.

If you don't hit your outcome goals, you may not only feel anxiety but also disappointment. On the other hand, when you are focused on an execution goal, you are in the moment with the process, and you are not bringing the judging mind or the critic into the equation.

When you are focused on improving, you will *keep* improving, and you are more likely to hang in long enough to start seeing the results reflected in your outcome goals.

Personal Best

Being driven is a natural part of being an entrepreneur. But when growing a successful, profitable business, you are going to fail somewhere along the way. If your sole focus is on gaining market share, you will be motivated for a while, but it will not take you the full distance to reach your goals. To remain truly motivated for the long run requires shifting your focus from business growth to your own growth and improving your effectiveness.

Don't get me wrong—growth and profit are important, but those are outcome goals. Having every endeavor succeed is just not within your full control. Hitting your revenue and growth goals are a gigantic boost to self-esteem, but if you judge your capabilities by reaching those numbers and you don't hit those numbers over and over again, you might lose confidence.

Comparing your business and how it is doing to similar businesses has a purpose: it lets you know where you stand. Gaining market share is important for success.

Your business may be getting known, but when this occurs too easily, it can lead to complacency and lack of focus. It is a double-edged sword.

The shift from gaining market share to gaining personal excellence sets you up for success. Setting goals to improve your personal skill set provides immediate feedback at the end of each and every day. You might not receive an award of recognition, but noticing improved effectiveness builds confidence and strengthens drive. With this mindset, even failing can be a strong motivator to succeed. Combine that with the commitment to do whatever is necessary to improve, and you become even more effective.

When you keep your focus on your personal best, you are always competing against yourself and never against others in your industry. New ventures and milestones then become opportunities to push yourself to go beyond where you are now.

Interestingly, stopping comparisons to the competition and instead focusing on improving your effectiveness is the fastest way to begin positioning your business for growth. You do have to keep in mind that stretching yourself means you risk failure or a setback, so you have to be willing to fail and to view those failures as learning opportunities.

As I mentioned earlier, introducing a new skill set or activity into your routine can often lead to a setback or failure. Your productivity may temporarily get a little worse because your brain is rewiring itself, creating new neuropathways as it sets the framework for moving forward again.

You are creating the opportunity to excel beyond where you are now, so your brain's ability to respond needs some time to get ready to implement the new approach, concept, or strategy. But if you are aware of that process and are patient with yourself, you will experience the leap in your effectiveness that makes it all worthwhile.

How to Change

As you integrate the material in this book, keep your focus on the execution goal of *improving* instead of having a specific outcome. I know this is a challenge. We have been conditioned to focus on outcome goals, but unless you pair them with performance milestones along the way, they will work against you in the long run.

This work is a process, a practice. It is unlikely that you will read this now and the next time you review your strategy, you will have a whole new approach to your business growth plan. Let's face it—you have been working in your business one way for a long time, and it takes time to integrate new systems and develop new habits. I acknowledge that change is easier for some people than for others, and we all have our own timelines for it. The key is to be open to change, however long it takes you to make it.

Recognize that how you do *anything* is how you do *everything*. If you stop yourself from improving your effectiveness, where else are you stopping yourself? Remember the businesswoman I spoke to who was facing confidence issues in her business? She came to me because she was fed up and finally willing to change.

The good news is that the reverse is true as well—if you change how you do *something*, that change will reverberate in all areas of your life.

A Model to Help You Change

To help you decide what changes to make, I suggest you apply the following criteria, which is based on the Stages of Change model by Prochaska, DiClemente, and Norcross. The researchers studied how people make changes in their life, whether consciously or unconsciously, and found that when people go through the following process, they are more likely to actually make the changes and to have longer-lasting results.

1. Pre-contemplation stage. In this stage, ask yourself if you even have an issue or a problem. For instance, did you resonate with the material about outcome versus execution goals? Is your focus on outcome goals a problem for you? If it is not a problem, you are not even going to consider making any changes.

2. Contemplation stage. If you have passed the first stage and you think the material could help you but you are not sure, do some research. This is an education phase. This book itself could be part of your contemplation stage about whether changing your mindset and limiting beliefs could be helpful to you.

3. Preparation stage. In this stage, you develop your game plan. You have decided that the change is a good idea, and now you want to think about how you could use the approach and make it work for you.

4. Action stage. This is when you start implementing the new approach. The action stage takes a lot of energy because you are focused on whether or not you are actually using the new approach. If you realize you are not, you take corrective action to put it into practice again. This stage has a learning curve and is largely trial and error.

5. Maintenance stage. You have incorporated the new approach into your routine or strategy, and it is easy now because you are used to it. You have a new behavior, a new approach, and a new mindset.

Take Personal Responsibility

When you make the choice to bring something into your routine or activity rather than a more passive approach in which you avoid a decision, you become more involved in your results and have more of a sense of ownership of it. This changes how you see yourself.

Your self-confidence rises. When your self-confidence rises, your effectiveness likely improves because you start taking actions that you might not have taken when you were more passive. There is also a shift in the dynamic with your associates or network. You become partners with the people supporting you.

I urge you to be active in your success. If your aspirations are to be the best you can possibly be, then you must take personal responsibility for your outlook and actions. Don't blame the economy, your network, or your technology system.

If your mentor tells you to do something and it is not necessarily the best way for you to get results, you have an obligation to yourself, your goal, and your actions to either figure out how to make the guidance work for you or approach that person with what you think is the better route. If you do the latter, together you might see if what you were told to do can be expanded on or adapted so that you can gain from it after all.

The Opportunities Are Already There

One of the many advantages to being active in your success is that you are more likely to recognize opportunities. The truth is, when you are looking to advance your business, the way to do it is already available to you, and it has probably been there all along. You just haven't been ready for it until now, so you haven't seen it, or maybe you didn't see it as an opportunity. You might have seen it as something fearful and avoided it.

For example, I was working with a group of entrepreneurs who were preparing to pitch their business idea to a panel of angel investors, and they told me that they were nervous talking about their concept. I suggested that they become comfortable with what seemed uncomfortable, and the way to do that was to register for practice pitch sessions offered by the local business development center because that would give them an opportunity to present their concept before a panel of business owners. It would take away the emotional charge, and they would also receive feedback on their presentation. This group of volunteer business owners on the panel work with emerging business owners on a regular basis and view the panel as an opportunity to pass it forward.

When I presented the idea, the new entrepreneurs initially resisted. They were concerned that the panel would criticize their business ideas. I pointed out that those business owners were once start-ups themselves, and if they approached them from the standpoint of wanting to learn from them, the panel of business owners would see it as mentorship and be willing to help them with their pitch. If they take my advice, the entrepreneurs will learn that they can face their fears, and by facing them, the fears will lose their power. This is a very simple solution to their problem, but it did require the entrepreneurs to be honest with me, and they will have to ask for help.

The opportunities around you are probably similar. They likely require you to face a fear or two and be open to looking at a situation in a new way.

Leaving Your Comfort Zone Is Liberating

Whenever we view something as an obstacle, whether consciously or not, we put a lot of energy into avoiding it. That is why I urge you to view obstacles as opportunities.

It opens you up to the simple solution that has been staring you in the face all along. It also opens you up to personal growth. When you view your obstacle as an opportunity, you head straight for it, facing what you need to face and growing in the process.

For instance, early in my coaching business, I recognized that I was holding myself back from opportunities because I didn't know if I would perform them well. I was concerned about being judged. That was not helping me to become a better business coach.

Working on my internal obstacles was a liberating experience. My performance improved. I felt more confident. I was also seen differently by my colleagues, because no matter what I was asked to do—even though a part of me wanted to say no at first—I always showed up and did it.

I learned things about myself—about my fortitude, resilience, determination, and how driven I am—that I never would have known if I had just avoided those things and stayed in my comfort zone.

Decidig Which Opportunity to Embrace

Going back to personal responsibility for a moment, you don't necessarily say yes to every opportunity that comes along. Some might not be right for you at the time.

When an opportunity is presented to you, ask yourself if it is aligned with helping you progress toward your goals. If it is, and it feels like the time is right to do it, then step up to the challenge. If it is not going to help you reach your goals, you don't have to do it.

If fear is the determining factor of whether you take advantage of an opportunity, you end up with a pretty small life and career. That is not to say you don't consider the risks. Fear serves a purpose.

For instance, I won't skydive. I don't avoid all risk; I am just selective about the ones I take. Avoiding physically dangerous activities is a survival response for me. The thought of getting seriously hurt stops me. Proving something to myself by jumping out of a perfectly good plane is not on my bucket list.

You have to look at the fear. What is it about, really? Once you do that, it usually becomes clear whether it is a fear you want to respect.

Mindful Performance

Reflexively kowtowing to fear is a reaction to that fear. A pattern of behavior is probably influencing your response. When you are in reaction in general, some outside stimulant has activated your beliefs, thoughts, and emotions, and you then turn to behaviors you have had for a long time that might not be best suited for the situation at hand.

When you perform mindfully, however, you are in action, not reaction. Instead of relying on outworn behaviors, you rely on your attitude and your execution. You set yourself up for mindful performance by anticipating challenges that might come up and having a strategic plan for dealing with those situations.

If you think about it, much of the "unexpected" is actually somewhat predictable. It usually involves marketing, technology malfunctions, delays with your product launch, and so on. Just for the fun of it, if you want to see examples of those unexpected moments firsthand, go to Google.com and search for the worst problems for business owners. You will be amazed at what you discover. You can then use that information to your advantage. Come up with your emergency action plan now for what you would do should any of those worst-case scenarios happen to you.

Thoughtful preparation is the key to a quick recovery for the unexpected challenges entrepreneurs experience as they advance. When you think through what might happen during your growth cycle and develop a strategic plan to deal with them, you feel more prepared and confident. Then, when something unexpected does occur, it doesn't throw you off. In fact, you will feel empowered and relaxed. When you are relaxed, you are better able to use the critical thinking skill of looking at all the options and coming up with the best solution.

Even if the situation isn't exactly the same as the ones you anticipated, it will likely be similar enough that you will be able to choose how you want to respond instead of falling into an automatic reaction.

Unexpected life events can occur without warning. For example, I decided to host an interview series, and completed all of the interviews one month before airing the series. Right after I started a month-long marketing campaign for the series, a family crisis occurred. This took me away from my business for three weeks.

The only option I had was to turn everything over to my assistant, releasing all control. I could have postponed the series because of the family emergency, but other commitments made that impossible. I also knew that this family issue needed my full attention and that I would be offline, so I just decided to pass the marketing plan on to my assistant and trust her to manage the details.

The truth is, I could have easily gotten all worked up, since others were depending on me to launch this series on time, but I had my back-up plan and enough insight about how to delegate each part of the marketing campaign, and everything happened according to schedule. My experience and my back-up plan prepared me for this particular situation even though I had never been in one like it before.

Just the process of thinking things through can help you avoid panic when the unexpected happens, because you are in the habit of thinking critically and looking for solutions.

Using the quicksand analogy, you may not know what to do, but if you don't panic, you might be able to see a way out of the quicksand. There might be a branch nearby, and if you think critically, you might be able to find a way to get that branch. If you are in a panic or are highly anxious, you don't have access to your critical thinking skills.

Will You Go for the Brass Ring?

I have covered a lot of ground in this book, but the bottom line is this: Will you decide to go for the brass ring?

In the olden days, merry-go-rounds had brass rings placed along the edge of the structure, just out of reach. If you grabbed a brass ring, you earned a prize. To grab the ring required a literal stretch as well as a stretch of your comfort zone because you might fall off the horse. But if you could strategize and time it correctly, and try a few times, you could figure out exactly the right timing and angle of reach to be able to reach out far enough, grab the ring, and stay on your horse.

Before you grab the ring, however, you have to make the decision to attempt it. You have to ask yourself: Is this an opportunity for me or not? Once you decide to reach for the brass ring, your brain will start to look for the opportunities to help you stretch yourself and grab hold of it. But it all begins with a decision.

Are you going to grab the brass ring? Are you going to be more open to opportunities? Are you going to turn the page and take the first step? Are there things you could be doing to improve your effectiveness that you are not doing yet? Is having a temporary setback in order to take a great leap forward in the long run worth it?

People who are afraid of disappointing themselves or others or of making mistakes are not as likely to push themselves or step forward in that way, because their inner critic is telling them all the reasons why they shouldn't. Successful entrepreneurs push forward anyway. They see the opportunity to improve their effectiveness as just the next step toward reaching their goals. They get excited by the challenge.

How do you view challenges? Do they bring up fear or apprehension? Do they bring apprehension and then action? Or do they just motivate you to take action? Obviously, the third response is preferable, but as I have discussed throughout this book, change is possible. Change begins with a decision. You can choose to change your approach and take action on things that you wouldn't have taken action on until now.

You Are a Success

If you really want something and you know in your heart that it is what you ought to be doing, then stay true and committed to it, no matter what anybody else says. Your conviction and your connection to your Big Why, your motivator, will take you the distance.

Whether or not you actually reach your loftiest goal, you will meet others along the way. The fact that you took action and a no-excuses approach will make you a success, and you will end up being a better person all around because of that choice.

11: Your Next Step

Many people go to seminars and read books that provide a lot of information, but then they get overwhelmed because the book or seminar didn't tell them how to get started, so they don't start anywhere. I want to make sure that doesn't happen to you, so here is your first step:

Get a piece of paper and write "GOAL" at the top. (This exercise is included on the bonus page at http://BusinessSuccessSolution.com/book-bonus.) Then down the left side of the page, go letter by letter and answer the following questions.

G is for your goal. What do you want to achieve by a particular point in time?

O is for all the obstacles in the way of that goal. What are the "yes, buts," the excuses and reasons why you shouldn't be trying to achieve your goal? You may say these things to yourself, or other people may say them to you.

A is for all the possible action steps you can take to reach your goal. Before you do this step, read the beginning of chapter 10 again for my suggestions of the most important changes to make right away. Let yourself imagine what they might be. Don't censor yourself; you are not committing to anything yet. You are just letting your mind be free to find possible solutions you have never thought of before.

L is your list of one to three of the action steps you are willing to commit to and take now.

The final result might look like this:

G O A L

G: My goal is to launch my new product and achieve 30 percent growth over the next twelve months.

O: Obstacles include the fact that I don't see eye to eye with my business partner. My computer crashed, I used my reserve cash to replace it, and I am still not 100 percent recovered. I hold back because I am afraid of failure. I don't have the money to invest in getting a booth at industry conferences.

A: Possible action steps include taking Loren's advice and talking to my business partner to try to bridge an understanding between us. I could work through my fear by using EFT. I could reach out to clients who still owe me money about collecting on their past due bills. I could research highly successful entrepreneurs in my profession to see what they do different from me. I could stop saying I don't have the money and look around for creative ways to attend industry conferences. For instance, I have a lot of cousins in major cities I could stay with while I went to a conference. I could apply to speak at a conference or network without a booth.

L: The action steps I will take right away are to talk to my business partner, practice with EFT by using the sample for fear in the appendix of this book, and call clients about their past due bills.

Now you do the same, right now, before you close this book. Give yourself the gift of starting on this new path toward your goal. All you have to do is begin. Remember, once you make the decision to commit to your goal, opportunities will start to appear. Try it for yourself and see.

If you would like more help or support, I set aside five complimentary strategy sessions each month. See the details on the next page.

Your Complimentary Grow-Your-Ideal-Business Strategy Session

Congratulations on making the choice to step out of the box and look for a new approach to improving your effectiveness.

You read this book because you are committed to being the best you can possibly be. Reaching your goals is important to you, and you are ready to do everything possible to be a highly successful entrepreneur. You stayed with this book because you knew the information here would give you insider tips used by the most successful business owners.

It is your turn to *take decisive action* so I can teach you how to build confidence, improve your focus, and effectively deal with distractions, plus everything else you need to create a success mindset. Now is the time to bridge the gap between what you *know* and what you *do*.

Join Me for Deeper Training

Success is more than just knowing what you are supposed to do. It is about taking action. I am highly dedicated to your success and want to offer you more than I could fit into this book.

Here is what you will get from the Grow Your Ideal Business Strategy Session:

• You will discover exactly what is stopping you from attracting clients and money.

- You will create a clear plan that describes the steps you need to take to launch your business to the next level.
- You will learn the one simple step you can take immediately to get into action!

If you have questions, just ask. Ask questions. It really is that simple. You will be amazed at how much we can cover during our conversation. No challenge is too small or too big or too tough. I promise you, I won't hold anything back. I will freely share what you can do now to advance your business. Then, if you are interested in working more closely together, we can discuss those options, as well.

As you put my suggestions into place, you will achieve more than if you attempt to figure out all the details out on your own. Success is all about implementation and fine-tuning for steady progress, and consistent effort will lead to breakthroughs. As you evolve, your business will grow—the bottom line is your results.

My Promise

I know you are busy, and I value your time. After our time together, you will leave the session renewed, re-energized, and inspired.

Let's work together on:

1. Thoughts and beliefs
2. Goals and vision
3. Action steps
4. Program, pricing, and sales
5. Leadership and communication
6. And more!

An Additional Special Bonus

I am always adding new trainings for my clients. For instance, if you like EFT but you are not sure what words to say, you can access my latest video on doing EFT on specific challenges. In fact, if you have a specific challenge and want to do EFT on it, let me know, and I might do a special tapping video on your issue. The videos are like having me do EFT right there with you. I will help you know what to say and how to do the tapping, and all you have to do is follow along. It is that easy!

As you know, a good coach can make all the difference in your success. Your mental game is the key to how well you will follow through with your strategy and action plan. A strong mindset is necessary for remaining focused under pressure. If you are tired of delaying your decision to grow your ideal business, then I encourage you to apply for one of these limited strategy sessions spots right now. Please visit http://businesssuccesssolution.com/get-started/ to request a strategy session   .

Appendix I
EFT Instructions

You possess a variety of beliefs about your actions, abilities, and goals that were formed in various ways. Many were absorbed from your surroundings when you were a child, before you had the ability to choose your beliefs, and others were formed from experiences you have had since then. Many of these beliefs work to your advantage. Others, however, prevent you from achieving your full potential.

As you read in chapter 6, EFT (Emotional Freedom Techniques), or tapping, works with acupressure points in the body to help neutralize negative emotions around a specific event and correct the flow of energy. The process makes you conscious of limiting beliefs you have adopted and gives you the freedom to choose new beliefs.

To perform EFT, you tap with your fingertips on various acupressure points on your body as you focus on a particular emotional or physical issue. As you do so, balance is restored, often within minutes. It sounds simple and easy, and it is. It also works.

Here are the basics for how to use this powerful tool on yourself. You can also follow along with the bonus EFT videos at http://BusinessSuccessSolution.com/book-bonus.

The Tapping Points

The tapping points are at the ends of meridians on your body. Meridians are channels for energy where *qi* (chi), the circulating life force, flows through the body. Storing emotions in the body contributes to imbalance, which affects the flow of energy. Tapping on the ends of the meridians helps to balance out disruptions that exist in your energy system. The end points used in the tapping sequence are close to the surface of your body and are easily accessible.

Follow the tapping sequence below, and use all of the points. Although two people might address the same issue, the meridian that is blocked may be different for each one because of their individual experiences and perceptions. When you tap on all of the eight points, you actually access every meridian in your body and will hit the block each and every time without having to know which meridian is blocked. The goal is to successfully clear the energy so you can achieve performance results.

Note: When I tap, I like to use the four fingertips of my hands on each tapping point and never use my thumbs. I suggest using the same amount of pressure to tap as you do when you drum your fingers on a tabletop.

The Tapping Points and Sequence:

Here are the tapping points and sequence to do EFT:

Karate Chop Point: This is the setup point. Open one hand, and using the other hand's fingertips, tap on the outside edge of the open hand between your wrist and pinkie.

Eyebrow Point: This tapping point is located above each eyebrow. Place the fingertips of each hand over each eyebrow and tap directly above the eyebrows using all four fingers on each hand.

Sides of the Eyes: The next tapping point is the outer corners of your eyes. Use all four fingers of both hands on both eyes at the same time. Don't get so close to your eye that you are likely to poke it.

Under the Eyes: This point is on the cheekbones just below the eyes and in line with the pupils. Use all four fingers of both hands, and tap both cheekbones at the same time.

Under the Nose: Use only one hand for this point. Use all four fingers to tap above your lip, with your pointer finger tapping on the indentation under your nose.

Chin: Use only one hand for this point. Tap in the indentation between your lower lip and your chin.

Collarbones: The collarbone point is the most difficult one to get correct. Most people tend to tap too high up on their collarbones. The correct point is toward the center where your collarbone begins and then one inch down where you feel an indentation. Once again, use both hands to tap on each side of your collarbone. Refer to the diagram below.

Under the Arms: This tapping point is located about four inches under the arm pits. Cross your arms as if giving yourself a hug when tapping on this point. Another variation is to tap with the fingers of the hands on the same sides of the body. Either way is fine; do whatever is most comfortable for you.

Top of the Head: This is the final point used to complete the tapping sequence. With one hand, tap on the crown of your head.

How to Use the Tapping Sequence: The Short-Cut Method

Part of my approach includes identifying the first event during which a limiting belief was probably formed. I then begin to address the original circumstance and to shift the perception concerning it. This helps to clear the presenting problem.

For now, however, just think about an obstacle that is affecting your business. Some suggestions include having physical pain or anxiety or not feeling confident. After you choose an issue, get as specific as you can about the circumstances under which it occurs.

1. Rate the intensity. Before you start tapping, rate the intensity of that issue on a scale from 0 to 10, with ten being the most intense.

2. Perform the setup. While continuously tapping the Karate Chop point only, repeat this affirmation three times:

"Even though I have this [name your obstacle], I deeply love and accept all parts of myself."

3. Do the tapping sequence. Now tap seven times on each of the energy points described previously as you repeat a reminder phrase at each point. A reminder phrase is a short statement that is related to the setup affirmation in Step 2.

In the examples that follow, you will notice that sometimes the reminder phrase changes for each point. This is helpful but not necessary for success. Your reminder phrase can be very simple and stay the same for each tapping point.

Let's do the sequence together, as shown below. [1] Say you get nervous right before presenting to a group, to the point where you are sick to your stomach. First, we will do the setup together on the karate point chop. You will repeat the setup phrase three times. Then will start tapping on each point while saying a reminder phrase. In the example here, you will repeat the phrase

---

[1] Illustration by Gloria Arenson, MFT, author of Five Simple Steps to Emotional Healing, Freedom at Your Fingertips, and Born to Spend. Used with permission.

"sick to my stomach" while tapping on all the points in sequence.

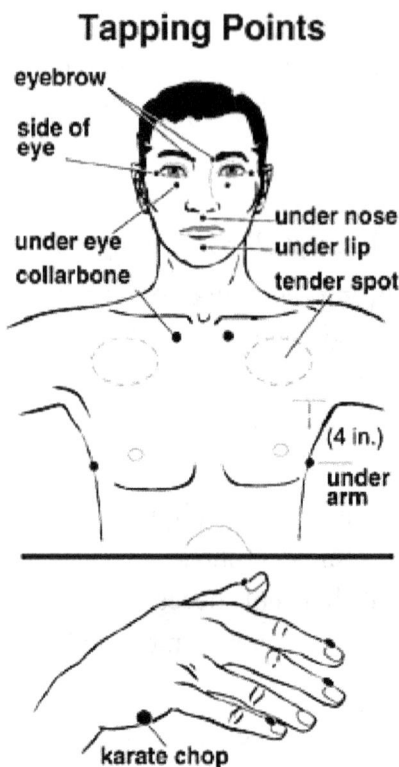

Tapping Points

eyebrow

side of eye

under eye

collarbone

under nose

under lip

tender spot

(4 in.)

under arm

karate chop

Even though we are keeping it simple, your subconscious mind will be attuned to what is going on and will work with you to calm you down right before the presentation.

Setup: "Even though I have this sick feeling in my stomach, I deeply love and accept all parts of myself." Repeat three times while tapping the Karate Chop point.

Eyebrows: Sick to my stomach.

Sides of eyes: Sick to my stomach.

Under eyes: Sick to my stomach.

Under nose: Sick to my stomach.

Chin: Sick to my stomach.

Collarbones: Sick to my stomach.

Under arms: Sick to my stomach.

Top of head: Sick to my stomach.

4. Take a deep breath!

5. Rate your ending intensity from 0 to 10. Are you still at the same number as when you began, or did the number change? Did the level of intensity go up or down? Recall whether any specific thoughts, memories, or sensations occurred while you were tapping. If so, that is good and is seen as progress.

If the intensity is above a 2, repeat the tapping sequence. If appropriate, you can make the following changes:

• Make the statement more specific. What is the best way to describe what you are feeling now, after the tapping?

• Modify the setup statement to "Even though I still have some of this _____, I deeply love and accept all parts of myself." For example, you did the sequence, and you don't feel quite as sick to your stomach as you did before, but your stomach is still queasy. For this next round of tapping, you can say the following setup three times before you begin tapping: "Even though I have this remaining sick-to-my-stomach feeling, I deeply love and accept all parts of myself."

• Say a slightly modified reminder phrase as you tap all the points again. For example, your reminder phrase might now be "remaining upset stomach" on each tapping point.

Let's do it together once more.

Setup: "Even though I have this remaining sick-to-my-stomach feeling, I deeply love and accept all parts of myself." Repeat three times.

Eyebrows: remaining upset stomach

Sides of eyes: remaining upset stomach

Under eyes: remaining upset stomach

Under nose: remaining upset stomach

Chin: remaining upset stomach

Collarbones: remaining upset stomach

Under arms: remaining upset stomach

Top of head: remaining upset stomach

A Variation to Try

In the example below, we use different reminder phrases for each point. If you would like to try it, think about an execution goal you want for yourself but feel a resistance to or a barrier around it. Notice whether you feel the resistance somewhere in your body. Rate your physical or emotional feeling on a scale between 0 and 10.

Now we tap on the Karate Chop point for the setup. Notice that it is okay to include variations on the affirmation when you repeat it three times—or you may keep it the same.

This time, after we do the setup, we will do two consecutive rounds of tapping.

Set up: Even though I continue to have this part of me that resists change, I deeply and completely love and accept all parts of myself.

Even though this vulnerable part of me is satisfied with how things are now and I don't understand this, I accept who I am and how I feel.

Even though I spend a lot of time preparing and delay getting started, I deeply and profoundly accept all of me—even the part that is resisting change and distracts my focus.

Now tap on each point seven times, using the reminder phrases below.

Eyebrows: Wouldn't it be nice if I could always maintain my focus?

Sides of eyes: The thought of feeling focused and confident is appealing.

Under eyes: I remember a time when I was doing what was necessary and the energy I felt from that.

Under nose: There continues to be a part of me that is comfortable with where I am now.

Chin: I don't understand that part of me.

Collarbones: That is okay.

Under arms: I accept all parts of me right now.

Top of head: I choose to accept every part of me, no matter what.

Eyebrows: I appreciate all aspects of who I am.

Sides of eyes: Even the parts of me that resist and distract my focus.

Under eyes: I appreciate how I think and my desire to succeed.

Under nose: Even when I get overwhelmed and become distracted.

Chin: I appreciate every single part of me.

Collarbones: Even though the resistance to change is stronger than I would like. It appears to be protective, though.

Under arms: I choose to accept all of me.

Top of head: I choose to accept all parts of me, no matter what.

Take a deep breath. Check in, and see if the number of the intensity you had has changed. If you felt the resistance in your body somewhere, is it still there? Did it change or move? Any movement is positive, even if it becomes more intense. Movement means change is beginning to happen.

If you are not at a zero level of intensity, I recommend you do the tapping sequence again. Remember to make it even more specific to the particular issue you have regarding resistance to see if that helps clear it for you.

The Emotional Freedom Techniques have the ability to remove the barriers to your progress. Using this process will help you reach your execution goals quickly and more easily. Be skeptical, but give it a try. In fact, try it for everything. The benefit of using the Emotional

Freedom Techniques is the ease of shifting your mindset from negative to positive.

On the following pages are several specific EFT examples you can model as you learn to use the technique. Again, you will notice that some of them use different reminder phrases. Feel free to model them, or use just one simple reminder phrase.

Appendix II
EFT Sample to Neutralize Anxiety

One of the biggest complaints about EFT is that it focuses on negative emotions. That is true. Too often, people want to tiptoe around negative things because they are uncomfortable. Identifying the negative and saying the words aloud reduces the intensity of the emotion, and the negativity begins to lose its power. It is similar to revealing a deeply held secret you were embarrassed about. Once you share the secret with someone and they don't judge you about it, you feel a sense of relief. You suddenly feel free from something you had spent a lot of time avoiding.

Having said that, I don't like negativity, either, so when I use EFT, I do two rounds in consecutive order. First I do a round on the negativity, then I do a round on the positive, reinforcing the change I am working toward. We will do that together now.

Think of a time when you felt anxious, even in a near panic, about an action. Remember how it distracted you, affecting your focus, and the way your body felt when those thoughts flooded through your head.

Now feel that anxiety as if it were happening right now. Give that anxiety a rating from 0 to 10, with 10 being a panic attack and 0 being fully relaxed. Do you feel the anxiety in your body? Where? What does it feel like? While you still have those feelings, begin tapping on the Karate Chop point for the setup.

If the words I use in the example are not right for you, substitute your own to fit your experience. Notice that this example uses a more complex style for its reminder phrases.

While tapping on the Karate Chop point, say these words aloud:

"Even though I have *big* goals for myself, a part of me is not sure about success, but I deeply love and accept all parts of myself.

"Even though I really want to be successful with my business just as I dreamed, I continue to have this nagging feeling that I don't deserve success. Now I choose to focus on my gifts and the goals I have set for myself.

"Even though I feel selfish focusing on what I want and what I need to succeed, I truly believe this is the path for me to follow."

Now tap on each of the points as you repeat the words, or you may use the simple phrase of "doubts about success" for each point:

Eyebrows: I know what I would like to have, but is it possible?

Sides of eyes: There is so much work I need to do to reach my goal.

Under eyes: I am already overwhelmed.

Nose: I can't add anything else to my plate.

Chin: What if I am not able to meet other people's expectations?

Collarbones: I am not really sure I can pull it off.

Under arms: I don't know if I deserve to be doing this.

Top of head: Now is not the time to feel this way. I already feel like I have to do so much to get ahead and get noticed.

Now let's focus on the positive:

Eyebrows: I can easily imagine being a success.

Sides of eyes: When I stop and think of being a success, it feels so right.

Under eyes: Being in the moment helps to keep me focused on the *big* picture.

Nose: I choose to embrace the feeling of success and know I have earned it.

Chin: I have what it takes to be a success.

Collarbones: Getting clear about how I am going to help my clients feels so right.

Under Arm: Visualizing my success lifts my vibration.

Top of head: When I feel confident about this path I am taking, my vibration rises and attracts opportunities to me.

Take a deep breath.

Visualize your success. Really see yourself as having achieved your goal. Make it as real as you possibly can by bringing all of your senses into play. See it, feel it, be it. Create a success mindset laser focused on reaching your highest potential.

Appendix III
EFT Sample to Neutralize Fear

I use EFT on myself as well as with my clients. When I first started my business, my business coach told me I was going to learn to love public speaking. I just chuckled. She had no idea what I thought about public speaking and networking.

Once I made the choice to step out of my comfort zone and give speaking a chance, I knew change was going to happen. A complete overhaul in my thinking about speaking and networking was necessary.

There was nothing I could change about speaking to a group of business owners. What I chose to do was change my perception and beliefs about speaking. I had to get honest with myself. It was time to figure out what I was avoiding and what was holding me back. There was a disconnect between what I wanted for myself and how I felt about doing those things. The fear factor was strong. Do you ever feel that way?

Think of a time when you felt fear about your business, about being expected to do something and didn't feel you could pull it off. As the thoughts were going through your mind, did you want to avoid it? Did you procrastinate, or did you white-knuckle your way through?

Now feel that fear as you did when you faced that challenging activity. Give that fear a rating between 0 and

10, with 10 being extreme fear and 0 being confident. What number do you give it? Do you feel it anywhere in your body? If so, where? What does it feel like?

While you still have those feelings, we will begin tapping on the Karate Chop point as we do the setup. Again, if the words I use are not quite right, substitute your own words to fit your experience.

While tapping the Karate Chop point, say these words aloud or use your own:

"Even though I want to take on the challenge before me right now, I know something is holding me back, but I deeply love and accept all parts of myself.

"Even though I know what needs to be done to meet the expectations, I have a lot of excuses for why I can't do it right now. I know this is how I feel and will take action when I am ready.

"Even though I am the only one keeping me from taking action and I feel the weight of my resistance, I know what I need to do and am working toward the time when I will move forward with confidence and ease."

Now tap on the sequence of points while repeating these words:

Eyebrows: I have a self-imposed glass ceiling holding me back from reaching my full potential.

Sides of eyes: I know what I need to do, but I am resistant to doing it.

Under eyes: I am afraid to push myself.

Under nose: I know all the reasons and excuses for not taking action now.

Chin: There is a price to pay for success, and I am not sure I am willing to pay that price.

Collarbones: What will I have to leave behind if I reach the next level of success?

Under arms: Just thinking about everything I have to do and what will need to change is overwhelming.

Top of head: What if I fail?

Again:

Eyebrows: I have the ability to change my focus and look at what I am moving toward.

Sides of eyes: I have always had this vision, and I feel the time is right for making a decision about excellence.

Under eyes: When I visualize reaching my goal, I can feel my energy rise.

Under nose: I love the feeling of confidence and achievement I get when I focus on the positive.

Chin: I have so much to offer, and now is the time to claim my place with purpose.

Collarbones: I know what I need to do and am ready to do it now.

Under arms: My heart and my head are in the right place. I feel really clear about my purpose.

Top of head: The vibration of being a success is motivating. I know I have the ability to rise up to and overcome any challenge I create for myself. I love the feeling of confidence as I move forward with purpose.

Take a deep breath.

Change was possible once I knew my goal, my strategy, and my plan. My desire to succeed, to help growth-minded entrepreneurs get out of their own way to succeed, was greater than my fear. It was time to face my fears head on. I had all the tools available to get past my blocks, and the opportunity was right to make a change. I had to become comfortable with what had been uncomfortable up to this time. This was when I embraced the motto: "If it's uncomfortable, then I ought to be doing it."

Being compelled to stretch myself and then growing from the decision created the drive I needed to walk through my fear and resistance. Determination helped me to keep moving forward, even when it was uncomfortable. I reached a point in my life where I could not remain stuck any longer.

Appendix IV
EFT Sample: Money Blocks

I recently hosted a retreat for my business coaching clients. It focused on developing a strategic plan, and I was eager to help my clients clarify their goals. I am a results junkie and tend to think outside the box. Although I know my clients' abilities, I choose to stretch their vision so they advance at a faster rate than if they were doing this on their own.

That retreat was no exception. After the morning check-in, I wanted to set a clear intention for the day together. As soon as we completed the first activity, I knew several members felt their goals had stretched beyond their comfort zone. They wanted to back-pedal by choosing a more cautious outcome. The idea of growing too fast and achieving those results had raised underlying concerns about money and wealth for them. The downside to success caught them off guard.

This was the first time some of them had ever fully defined their vision of success. Although no one was beating themselves up over the flood of emotions, one person, whom I will call Lindsey, admitted she felt foolish. She expressed conflict and was unsure whether wealth would alter her values. She had never learned how to save money.

Several underlying thoughts had surfaced, which offered Lindsey an opportunity to explore her beliefs about money. We used EFT to work through her money block and began tapping on each of the points.

Lindsey and I did this EFT session in a room full of people. Instead of worrying about who saw us doing this silly tapping thing, the entire room joined in to experience the process. Tapping as a group is a wonderful way to support a specific individual. The added benefit is that others in the room may resolve a similar issue. Below is the setup and simple reminder phrases we used for each round of tapping.

Setup: "Even though I am not comfortable with earning too much money, I deeply love and accept all parts of myself." (Repeated three times.)

On each point, I used the reminder phrase, "Earning too much money." Then we tapped again, using this:

Setup: "Even though I want to grow my business and the money part is uncomfortable, I deeply love and accept all parts of myself." (Repeated three times.)

On each point, the reminder phrase was, "Money is uncomfortable."

Again:

Setup: "Even though I work hard to earn money, and money creates problems, I deeply love and accept all parts of myself." (Repeated three times.)

On each point, the reminder phrase was, "Money creates problems."

Then finally:

Setup: "Even though I could do more things if I had more money and I always spend what I have, I deeply love and accept all parts of myself." (Repeated three times.)

On each point, the reminder phrase was, "Spend what I have."

The entire room tapped steadily for about three minutes. Lindsey's money concerns gradually receded from an intensity of 10 out of 10 to a 3 and then to a 1. Several other people in the room also noticed some relief regarding their specific money blocks.

Finally, Lindsey was able to uncover her real concerns. More money would increase family expectations to share the money with them. At first she thought she had already worked through these issues, but this session uncovered a new layer of awareness.

Later, during a private session together, she did some more work on that issue. She focused on a time she earned babysitting money and her brother stole it from her.

We began with the setup phrases below.

"Even though I did babysitting to earn my money and wanted to buy new jeans with it, I deeply love and accept all parts of myself."

"Even though I was excited about using my own money to get new jeans, my brother stole my money. I deeply love and accept all parts of myself."

"Even though the money slipped through my hands and was taken from me, I somehow ended up getting blamed. I deeply love and accept all parts of myself."

On each of the points we used the reminder phrase, "My stolen money."

Other times when money had come into Lindsey's life, it never stuck around for long. After this specific round of tapping, her emotional intensity level was about 2 out of 10. Once again we began tapping. This time, I wanted to tap on the urge to quickly spend her money.

We began with the setup phrase below:

"Even though I spend money as quickly as I get it, I deeply love and accept all parts of myself."
(Repeated three times.)

On each point, we said the reminder phrase, "Quickly spend money."

Then we tapped again, using this:

"Even though I wanted to keep what I earned, I deeply love and accept all parts of myself." (Repeated three times.)

On each point, we said the reminder phrase, "Keep what I earned."

Then again:

"Even though I had worked hard for my money and then it was quickly taken away from me, I deeply love and accept all parts of myself." (Repeated three times.)

On each point, we said the reminder phrase, "Taken from me."

Then finally:

"Even though saving money is something I never do, I am open to the possibility that I can hold on to money. I deeply love and accept all parts of myself."

On each point, we said the reminder phrase, "Hold on to money."

Tapping with my clients on a specific issue works through blocks faster than traditional methods such as affirmations. The first thing Lindsey noticed was how her memory of her brother stealing her babysitting money didn't bother her anymore. Her anger had dropped down to a 0. She was pleasantly surprised that her anger had disappeared. Lindsey was encouraged to drink a lot of water that day to help recharge her energy.

The next week she checked in with me. A new client had given her a large payment to get started. The impulse to immediately spend the money didn't surface. Instead, she hired a bookkeeper to help manage her money.

Appendix V
EFT and Visualization Exercise

Note: Before doing this exercise, refer to the step-by-step instructions in Appendix I for how to perform EFT.

Below are specific steps to combine EFT and visualization. Remember, when you combine visualization with EFT, you get the benefits of both techniques.

1. Close your eyes. Breathe deeply and relax your body. Think about an upcoming activity that you have some anxiety about or an area in which you want to excel. Include as much detail as possible. What do you see? Where are you standing? Include smells and noises.

Some people are not able to visualize easily. That is okay. Just think about the activity in your mind.

2. Now do the EFT setup: while tapping on the side of your palm, say out loud, "Even though I don't feel confident doing this and am afraid that I will fail, I can choose to do this with confidence and ease." Repeat it twice.

3. Then rerun your visualization. Imagine yourself doing that activity successfully, and tap on all of the points. In your mental dress rehearsal, see, hear, and feel it happen as you always dreamed it could. See yourself engaged in that activity with confidence and ease. Imagine yourself feeling in control of the activity. As you continue tapping,

include all the details that might occur during this activity, and imagine that you are doing them all successfully.

During the visualization, did you have any doubts or thoughts that you could not do this activity successfully? Did you begin to feel anxious? That is okay. In fact, being aware of your doubts and apprehension is highly beneficial, because now you can use EFT to neutralize them.

Use EFT to Remove Doubts

If you had any doubts or anxiety arise when you did your visualization, you can use EFT to remove the negative feelings and energy that came up.

1. In this approach, called the Choices Method, you will focus on negative thoughts during the first round, positive thoughts during the second round, and then alternate between negative and positive thoughts on the third round. Model the following example.

Before we begin, tune in to the challenge and give yourself a rating on its emotional intensity from 0 to 10, with ten being the most intense and 0 being no intensity whatsoever. Do you feel that emotion in your body?. If so, where do you feel it? What does it feel like? Now let's get tapping, beginning with the setup on the Karate Chop point.

First round:

Setup: "Even though I feel anxious when I think about doing this and cannot believe that I can do this without anxiety, I choose to do this with confidence and ease."

Setup: "Even though the thought of doing this makes my heart race and I feel apprehension, I choose to do this with confidence and ease."

Setup: "Even though the thoughts I have about this are what make me feel anxious and uncomfortable, I have prepared for this successfully in my mental dress rehearsal and choose to do this with confidence and ease."

Eyebrows: This anxiety.

Sides of eyes: This anxious feeling.

Under eyes: I don't feel I can do this.

Under nose: I feel nervous just thinking about it.

Chin: I don't want to do this.

Collarbones: I am afraid I will mess up.

Under arms: This familiar nervous feeling.

Top of head: I feel anxious at the thought of doing this.

Continue tapping a second round:

Eyebrows: I can do this successfully in my imagination.

Sides of eyes: I can see myself doing this with confidence.

Under eyes: I know what I need to do.

Under nose: I have been preparing for this.

Chin: I can do this with confidence.

Collarbones: I know what I need to do.

Under arms: I am doing the best I can, given the circumstances.

Top of head: I feel proud that I am willing to change how I feel about this.

Finally, tap a third round:

Eyebrows: I am afraid that I will fail.

Sides of eyes: I know what I need to do.

Under eyes: I will forget what to do.

Under nose: I choose to know that I have prepared and rehearsed for this.

Chin: This familiar nervous feeling.

Collarbones: I can see myself doing this successfully.

Under arms: I don't want to do this.

Top of head: I choose to do this with confidence and ease.

Take a deep breath.

Now that you have done all three consecutive rounds, check in to see if your level of intensity has changed. Did it go up or down? Perhaps specific thoughts or memories occurred while you were tapping. If you are not yet at a zero, I suggest you do all three rounds again.

Practice this exercise anytime you have time to relax. When I cured my sugar addiction, I tapped twice a day for ten days. How long it takes varies from person to person. You may notice improvement after the first session, but do give it some time to work.

You can use these techniques in any situation, with any challenge, and with any type of memory, whether business related or not. I tap on everything.

Over time, you will notice a change in how you view challenges. You will begin to feel more empowered, and your outlook will be more positive.

Combining EFT with visualization can help you rise to any challenge that comes your way and reach your true potential.

www.ingramcontent.com/pod-product-compliance
Lightning Source LLC
Chambersburg PA
CBHW072308210326
41519CB00057B/3093